by Ann Gray

a BEAD Cornucopia

GPL **GEORGESON PUBLISHING LIMITED**

Mill Hill beads used in this book were supplied by Tiffanies Treasures

Published by Georgeson Publishing Limited
P.O. Box 100-667
North Shore Mail Centre, Auckland
New Zealand
Ph: 649 410 2079 Fax: 649 410 2069
Email: gpl@georgeson.co.nz Web site: www.georgeson.co.nz

ISBN NO. 0-9582105-7-8

© 2001Ann Gray

Editor: Prue Georgeson
Photography: Maria Sainsbury
Illustrations and Layout: Andreena Buckton - Noodle Design Corp.
Printed in New Zealand

page

Colour Plates

contents

introduction

I don't believe I ever saw my Grandmother without her beads. No doubt she was a notorious flapper girl in the 1920's. For a small child who liked to dress up her wardrobe and dressing table were sheer heaven.

By the time I was at Art College in Britain I not only wore beaded clothing, but created it also. Studying fashion design at Newcastle Polytechnic I worked extensively with beaded silk chiffon. I created early jewellery pieces on a bead loom and later learned and adapted hand held techniques to suit my own designs.

As an artist, working extensively with oil paints and pastels, colour is of paramount importance to me. I draw inspiration from many sources, including nature and different and ancient cultures.

I have been fortunate to travel a great deal and collect beads from all over the world. The lustre of beads and the many different shapes and forms available make them an exciting medium with which to work.

I like to take something out of its usual habitat and create a new dimension for it. Elegance and impact through colour, light and form are always the desired result.

I hope you have great pleasure both in the making and the wearing of the designs in this book.

Ann Gray,
Auckland,
New Zealand 2001.

General Notes - Beads

Man has adorned himself from the beginning of time. Originally natural stones and shells with weathered holes were used. Once the awl was invented, early man could drill soft stones, wood and seeds between the palms of his hands. The earliest recorded stone beads were found in Upper Egypt. These were chipped to shape and then rounded between harder flattened rocks. The Egyptian words used for amulet also mean protection. Obviously threading several beads together would increase the "protection" and make a whole necklace an extremely powerful talisman.

Beads have always been made from many different natural substances which have enjoyed popularity at different times through history. Amber was greatly prized by the Greeks who believed it was made from the essence of the sun's rays, solidified in the sea and cast upon the shores. As technology improved and a bow drill was developed beads were made from harder substances.

Queen Victoria made jet hugely popular as mourning jewellery after the death of Prince Albert. Jet is fossilized wood from the Monkey Puzzle Tree which grew 180 million years ago and with the invention of the precision lathe in the nineteenth century jet was able to be shaped and refined and a successful industry developed for its production. The most famous jet comes from Whitby in Yorkshire, England.

Many tribal beads are formed from seeds. I spent 18 months in Thailand where the Karen hill tribes use shiny white seeds on the jackets of the married women. Fondly called "Job's tears" they are a status symbol and sewn with various embroidery stitches into intricate patterns. During the year I spent in Java I found the "rudraksha" nut used for Hindu prayer beads, while many fruit seeds were dried, dyed and lacquered for necklaces and earrings.

Shells have also been widely used. Cowrie are perhaps the most well known, not only for adornment but also currency. Many cultures still consider cowrie to be a powerful fertility symbol and sew them along with glass seed beads onto matrimonial clothing.

Today the most popular beads are probably blown or wound glass. Hand painted Venitian beads were made famous by the Italian designer Fortuny in the 1920's and these are extremely valuable. But for general use, in most countries of the western world, we are fortunate that there are many beads of various sizes suitable for the designs featured in this book as well as artisans who make hand crafted beads for special designs.

Beads

Once you start to work with beads you will find they are very enticing. Not only do you have the excitement of choosing the colours and sheen of the beads which can be transparent, opaque, metallic, matt and iridescent you can also choose the shape and form. They are tactile and a pleasure to run through your fingers whilst working with them.

The majority of the beads used in this book are Mill Hill seed beads, which are readily available around the world and sold in small packets. The numbers of the packets have been given, colour names are an indication only. Although they are available in a selection of sizes I have used size 11 unless otherwise stated.

Designs

All the designs have very clear instructions and support diagrams to ensure that whatever you decide to make, you will enjoy the experience of creating your own unique art form. As a general guide the designs at the beginning of the book are simpler than those at the end of the book. The book is designed to lie flat in your lap for easy reference when working and the illustrations are repeated with each design so that there is no need to flick backwards and forwards through the pages when making one of the designs.

Thread

Beading is usually done with a very strong thread. The most commonly used thread is Nymo® which is available in a variety of colours. Choose the colour nearest to the colour of the beads you are working with.

Needles

Beading needs to be done with specialty beading needles. These are very fine as they have to fit through the hole in the bead several times depending on the pattern you are following. The higher the number the finer the needle. Needle lengths also vary, the shorter needles are often easier to use, especially when you are 'stitching' the main body of your beading whilst the longer needles are excellent for picking up long strings of beads for neckstraps or fringes.

Waxing

Waxing your thread is extremely important. Before you begin beading simply draw your thread several times through a block of beeswax. It is readily available from most beading and embroidery shops. This process not only strengthens the thread but also helps it to slide through the beads and avoid knots.

Keeper beads

A keeper bead is any bead tied on to prevent subsequent beads slipping off the end of the thread. It is tied on loosely so that it can be removed easily later (fig 1).

Fig 1

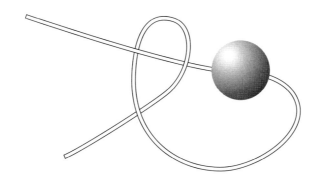

Fig 2

Turning bead

A turning bead is the name given to a bead on the end of a fringe. The thread is taken round the outside of the bead before going back through the bead next to it and returning up the fringe (fig 2).

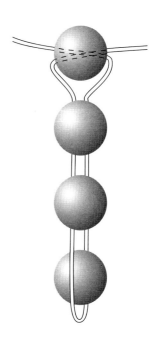

Attaching Clasps

When making a piece of jewellery with a clasp, remember to allow for the width of the clasp in the design. In the case of the magnetic clasps simply stitch around the clasp loop several times and then go through a bead in the necklace or bracelet strap and work a clove hitch and then repeat between several beads down the length. If one half of the clasp is a large ring for a bar or hook to go through, stitch the ring as above but before adding the bar it is advisable to add about three extra seed beads as this will facilitate fastening. Finish off the thread ends as above.

Starting and Finishing Threads

When finishing, bring in a new thread when the old thread is about 20cm (8") in length. (This leaves sufficient thread to finish properly.) To start the new thread wax then bring the thread up through a number of beads working catch stitches along the way so that the thread comes out in exactly the same position as the old thread. Carry on working with the new thread – this will enable you to keep the pattern correct (fig 3).

When you have worked a further dozen or so beads finish off the old thread.

To finish your thread at the end of a design take the thread back through half a dozen beads, work a clove hitch or little knot, repeat this two more times then take the thread back through a few more beads before snipping the thread end off.

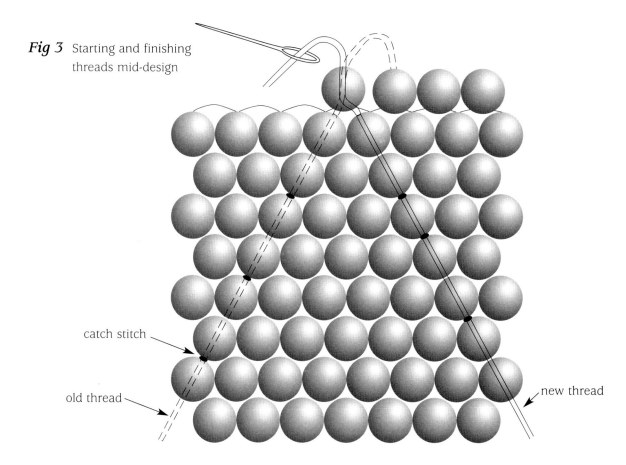

Fig 3 Starting and finishing threads mid-design

catch stitch

old thread

new thread

Following the Charts

Notes are given with the chart relating to each design. The starting point for each pattern is indicated by an arrow. The square stitch designs are worked down the chart and all other designs are worked up the chart. The starting position is indicated on each chart with an arrow.

Simple Beaded Necklace

refer to the colour photograph page 37

This elegant little necklace is as simple to make as it is delightful to wear. The beauty of the beads and simplicity of the design ensure that it enhances whatever you wear. The unusual shape of the beads used creates an interesting visual effect as the eye travels from the chunky angular beads to the smooth circular and cylindrical shapes.

There are many gorgeous beads available where simple threading is all that is required to show off the beauty of the beads. The threading technique remains the same whatever beads you use.

Materials

- 5g hematite 3mm (1/8") square beads
- 2g silver tubes 3mm (1/8") in length
- 5g hematite small tubes 2mm (1/8" approx.) in length
- 4.5g copper seed beads Mill Hill 00330
- 5g steel grey triangles 2mm (3/16") in length used in fringe only
- 1 x Antique gold clasp
- Nymo® thread to match
- wax
- beading needles

Technique -Threading

To Begin

Before starting to thread work out a bead pattern you like. Arrange the beads on a piece of velvet to avoid unwanted movement! This necklace is symmetrical so you only need to work out half of the design and repeat the second half as a mirror image.

I have a simple arrangement using four different beads. The main strand is threaded first. Cut a length of thread the desired length of your necklace (mine is 40cm, 16" not including clasps), allow an additional 40cms for finishing and to attach neck fastenings, wax well. To wax the thread simply pull it through a block of beeswax. This is readily available at beading and embroidery shops and strengthens the thread as well as helping it slide through the beads.

Tie on one copper seed bead as a keeper bead (see page 7 for more information on keeper beads). Then pick up several small beads (another copper seed bead, one hematite tube, a copper seed bead) as this makes the fastening of the clasp easier. To begin the pattern pick up the beads in the following order

9

*One hematite square, a silver tube, a hematite tube, a seed bead, a hematite tube, a silver tube and repeat from *until the necklace is the desired length. Finish with small beads to match the beginning and then tie a further keeper bead on until you are ready to attach the clasp.

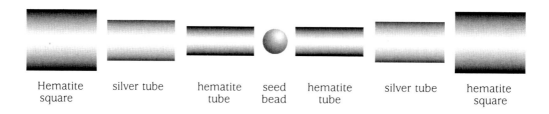

| Hematite square | silver tube | hematite tube | seed bead | hematite tube | silver tube | hematite square |

The Fringe Strands

To create the strands of fringe you will require a much longer piece of thread, a 1.5m (5ft) length is usually long enough and a good length to work with. Wax well.

Working from the *centre of your thread,* take your needle through the central bead of your necklace, in this case a copper seed bead, and add the middle fringing strand to it. The middle fringe is 4 cm (1 1/2") long and is made using a selection of the beads used in the necklace plus the steel grey triangles and turned on a copper seed bead. For more information on turning see page 7. The beads for the strands of the fringe are not arranged in the same order as on the main strand of the necklace, rather I have small beads down to larger, or large to small and back to large!

On completion of the first strand take your needle back through the central bead from the *opposite side you* began to ensure the fringe hangs correctly see fig 1 for the correct path for your needle, then take the needle through the beads to the correct starting point for the next strand of the fringe.
Continue making the fringes to one side, each fringe being 1 cm (1/2") or three beads from the previous one (or a measurement of your choice) and varying in length from 4cm (1 1/2"), to 3.5cm (1 3/8"), to 3cm (1 1/4"), 2.5cm (1") and 2cm (3/4") in length or length desired, always remembering to bring your thread out on one side of the bead in the main strand and take it back on the other side to ensure each strand of the fringe hangs perfectly.

When you have returned to the main necklace after the addition of the last strand of fringe on the first side of the necklace take the remaining thread back through the main necklace to the end working several clove hitches along the way. Attach one of the clasp pieces firmly then take the thread back through the main necklace to finish off the thread. Re thread needle with remaining thread, remove the keeper bead and attach it to the clasp also before finishing thread ends off in main necklace in the usual way.

Return to the centre of the necklace and working with the other half of your thread repeat the fringing instructions to create a mirror image of the first side. Attach the clasp to the other end in the same way, remembering to remove the keeper bead before attaching the clasp to the main thread. Finish thread ends in the usual way.

I am sure you will really enjoy wearing this beautiful necklace, a threaded necklace is so easy to make yet looks so good!

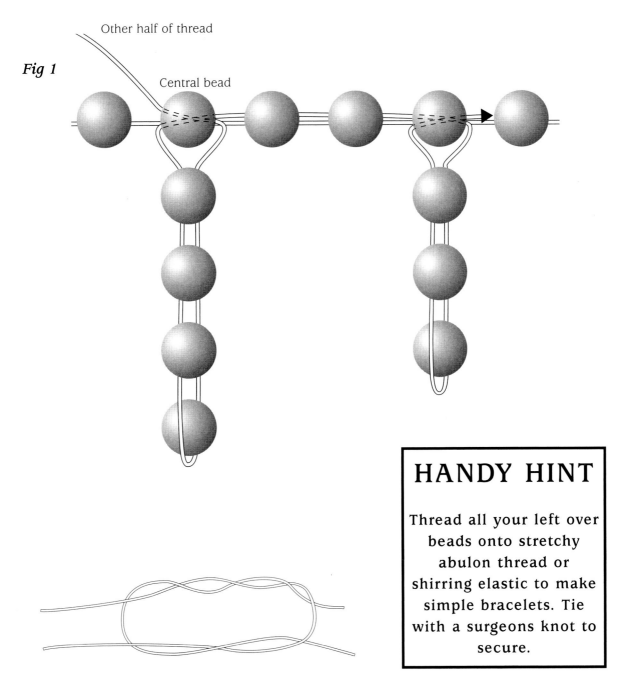

Fig 1

Other half of thread

Central bead

HANDY HINT

Thread all your left over beads onto stretchy abulon thread or shirring elastic to make simple bracelets. Tie with a surgeons knot to secure.

A surgeon's knot is a stronger version of a square knot. Left over right and around, then right over left and through. Go through the loop again then tighten.

Green & Gold Scroll Necklace

refer to the colour photograph page 39

Whenever I travel I am always on the lookout for exciting new beads. This necklace was inspired by the two green and gold bugles at the top of the square stitch design which remind me of ancient scrolls written on papyrus. The random pattern throughout the square stitching resembles ripples in the water by the banks where the papyrus grows.

Materials.

- Two patterned bugles 3cm x 0.5cm (1 1/8" x 3/8")
- 4.5g gold seed beads Mill Hill 00557
- 4.5g green seed beads Mill Hill 02020
- 28 x 2cm (3/4") twisted green bugles-*neckstrap*
- 6 x 6mm (1/4") glass lamp-worked beads with silver foil inserts-*neckstrap*
- 32 x gold beads size 6-*neckstrap*
- Nymo® thread to match

Technique: Square Stitch and Threading

Square stitch is a very satisfying stitch for a beading beginner to learn. It has the appearance of a loom worked piece and wonderful patterns can be developed as the beads line up vertically and horizontally. Square stitch is also incredibly strong as the thread is passed so often through the beads. In this design the square stitched panel is worked first and then the neckstrap is completed.

Row 1 To begin cut and wax a piece of thread 1.5m (5 ft) long.* Pick up a gold bead and tie it on as the keeper bead about 50cms (20") from the end of the thread. A keeper bead is tied on with a simple half knot *that can be undone later,* to prevent the other beads from slipping off the thread (see general notes page 7). Following the chart, thread the next 17 beads onto the thread, five gold, seven green, three gold and the last two green. (There are 18 beads in total in the row, the keeper bead is the first one.)

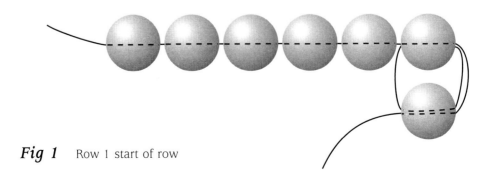

Fig 1   Row 1 start of row

12

Row 2 Pick up a green seed bead and stitch into the bead directly above it in a clockwise direction. Then take your needle back through the bead you have just added (fig. 1). Hold the beads firmly between your thumb and forefinger as you stitch so that the first bead in this row sits in the right position. From this point on follow the chart to keep the pattern correct. Pick up each bead and join it as shown (fig. 2). Continue in this manner across the row until you come to the gold keeper bead (the first bead in row one), undo the half knot before stitching into this bead.

When you have completed the second row, pass the needle through the previous row and back again through the beads of the row you have just stitched. This strengthens and stabilizes the work. Do this at the end of every second row also referred to as 'stabilizing thread'. It makes the beading very firm and strong. If however you prefer the beading to be more fluid this can be omitted.

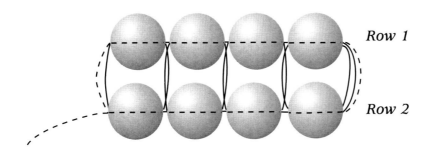

Fig 2 the dotted line shows the path of the stabilizing thread

Row 3 Pick up a green bead and stitch in an anti-clockwise direction through the bead at the end of the previous row (fig. 3). Following the chart continue in this manner to complete the third row. (You may prefer to turn your work around rather than work in an anti-clockwise direction, do whichever you find more comfortable.)

Fig 3

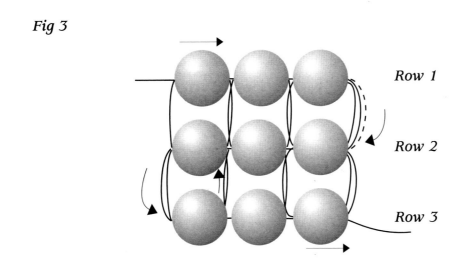

Following the Chart

The chart is worked from the top down and the rows are numbered. Arrows show the direction the rows are worked in.

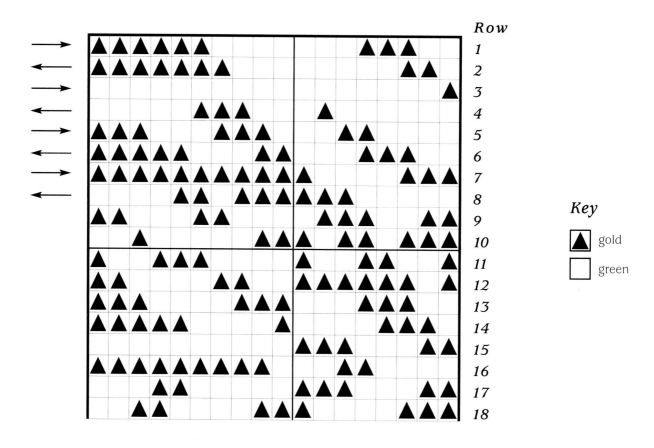

Key

▲ gold

☐ green

Rows 4 - 18 Work the remaining rows following the chart until it is complete. To fasten off, weave the thread through the beads working clove hitches in several places. (for more information on finishing see page 8.)

Return to the long thread end left at the beginning. Thread a needle and take it through the first patterned bugle then back through the first row of seed beads. Next take the thread back through the first bugle a second time and then through the second upper bugle for the first time, back through the first bugle again and the second bugle a second time (fig. 4). Work several clove hitches at the left hand edge of the work so the bugles cannot slip and then fasten off the thread end into the main body of seed beads in the usual way.

Fig 4

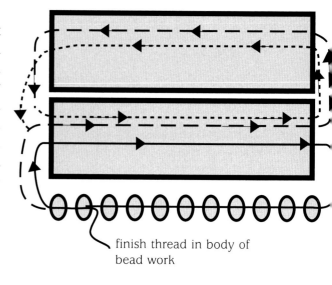

finish thread in body of bead work

The Neck Strap

The instructions given are for a neck strap with a finished length of 42cm (16 1/2") (not including clasps) when the necklace is laid out straight. To adjust the length add more or less bugle beads. Size 6 gold beads are used in the neckstrap. To make the neck strap cut and wax a 1.5m (5ft) length of thread. Secure the clasp in the centre of the thread by taking the thread through the clasp two or three times. Take both thread ends through two gold beads and then thread each end onto separate needles.

Thread each needle through a separate twisted bugle bead and then bring both needles together through two more gold beads (fig. 5). Do this three more times so you have four sets of bugles. This time thread both needles through one gold bead, then a glass bead with foil inset and another gold bead before the bugles. Do this two more times.

Thread on two more bugles, two gold beads and then take both needles through the patterned bugle bead at the top of your worked piece. Continue up the other side of the necklace working it as a mirror image of the first.
After your final two gold beads add three gold seed beads before attaching the bar section of the clasp. This helps the clasp to be fastened more easily. Work your thread end back down the necklace working two or three clove hitches to secure.

This stunning piece of jewellery will be a valuable addition to any wardrobe. Enjoy.

Fig 5

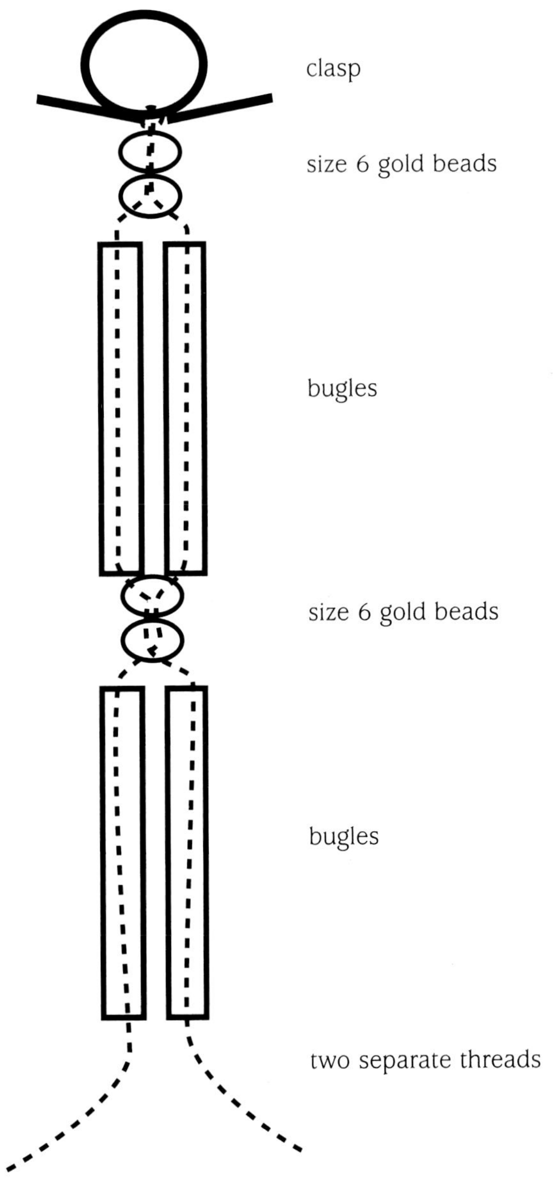

clasp

size 6 gold beads

bugles

size 6 gold beads

bugles

two separate threads

Bookmark

refer to the colour photograph page 37

This book mark has a wonderful fluidity that makes it a pleasure to run through your fingers! The design has a very bold, rather ethnic feel to it and whilst I have made it as a book mark it would be a striking necklace with the addition of a neck strap or a stunning brooch! Black and silver is a very arresting combination but others would also work well. Whatever you decide, it is a treasure anyone would be pleased to own.

Materials.

- 9g black seed beads Mill Hill 02014
- 8g silver seed beads
- Black Nymo® thread
- Wax
- Beading needle

Technique: Square Stitch

Instructions

The first two rows are worked using the black seed beads, from the third row on follow the chart for the pattern. To achieve a good final result tension is important, pull your thread firmly at all times.

Section 1

Row 1 Cut and wax a 1.5m (5ft) length of thread. Tie a black seed bead as a keeper bead about 20cms (8") from the end and pick up a further 16 black beads (for further information on keeper beads refer to page 7). Do not pull the beads too tightly at this stage.

Fig 1

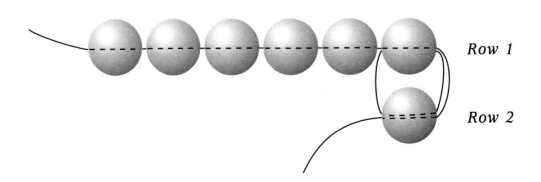

Row 1

Row 2

16

Row 2 This row is worked from right to left. Pick up a black bead and stitch clockwise into the bead directly above it. Then stitch back through the bead you have just picked up, (fig. 1). Pick up the next bead and repeat, stitching in a clockwise direction into the bead above and back through the same bead. Continue to the end of the row in this manner (fig. 2). When you reach the keeper bead at the end of the row, undo the half knot around the keeper bead and stitch into it. When you have completed the second row, pass the needle through the first or previous row and back again across the second or just stitched row. This strengthens and stabilizes the work. *Do this on the completion of every second row, also referred to as a 'stabilizing thread'. If you prefer your work to be more fluid you can leave the stabilizing thread out.*

Fig 2 the dotted line shows the stabilizing thread path

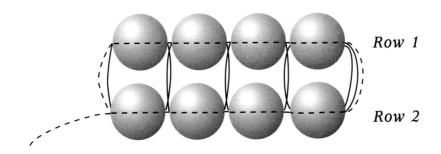

Row 1

Row 2

Row 3 Pick up a black bead and this time stitch in an anti-clockwise direction into the bead directly above. Stitch back through the bead you have just picked up. Continue in an anti- clockwise direction to the end of the row following the chart to keep the pattern correct (fig. 3).

Fig 3

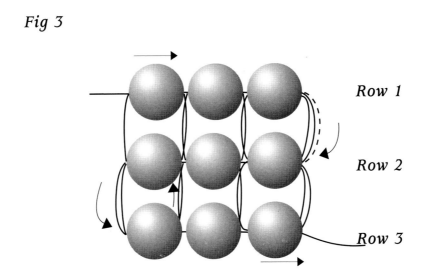

Row 1

Row 2

Row 3

17

Rows 4 - 15 Work these rows following the chart, remembering that the stitching direction changes each row from clockwise to anti- clockwise.
After completing the 15th row take your needle through the 14th row from right to left and through the first six beads of the 15th row.

Don't forget to take your stabilizing thread back through the last two rows of beading every second row. If you find it easier you can do it at the end of every row.

Section 2

Row 16 Pick up a black seed bead and stitch into the 6th bead along (fig 4), being careful not to change direction. Add the remaining six beads in this row, keeping the pattern correct.

Rows 17 - 21 For the next five rows one bead is added at each end of every row.
Row 17 Work across this row working into the seven beads from the previous row.

To increase (fig 4)
Pick up a black bead, this is bead 'A' and the first additional bead, pick up a further bead 'B' which is the bead which will be in row 18 below 'A'. Stitch back through A and B as shown. Continue the row as usual.

Fig 4

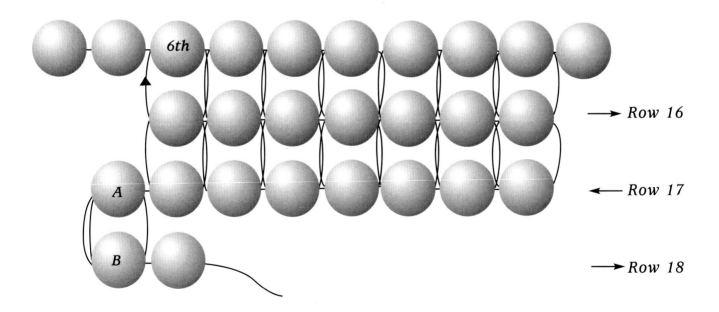

Following the Chart

The chart is worked from the top down and the rows are numbered. Arrows show the direction the rows are worked in.

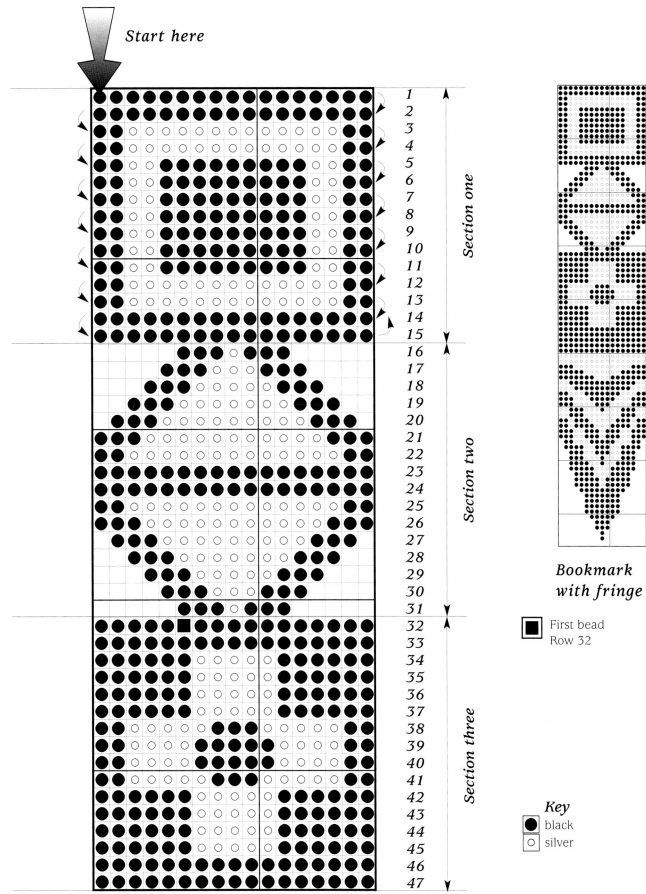

Start here

Section one

Section two

Section three

Bookmark
with fringe

First bead
Row 32

Key

● black

○ silver

– Bookmark –

At the end of the row add a further bead 'C' for this row and bead 'D' for the start end of the previous row (fig 5). Now take your thread back through rows 17 and 18, it will come out ready to continue at bead C (fig 5).

Fig 5

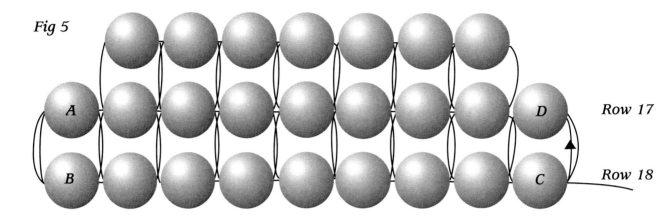

Row 17

Row 18

Pick up an extra bead for this row, plus an extra for the row below, beads 'E' and 'F' (fig 6). Continue in this way, following the chart until the work is 17 beads across once more.

Fig 6

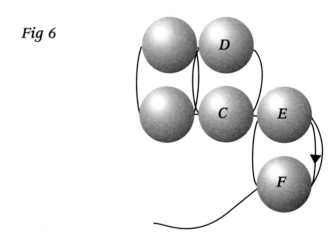

To Decrease (fig 7)
Now you will begin to decrease at each end of the row. This is much easier to achieve than increasing. Take your stabilizing thread through the previous row and the row just stitched but bring the thread out one bead before the end of the row. (fig 7). Turn the work and continue beading, ending one bead before the end of the row. Continue in this way until you are back down to seven beads.

FIg 7

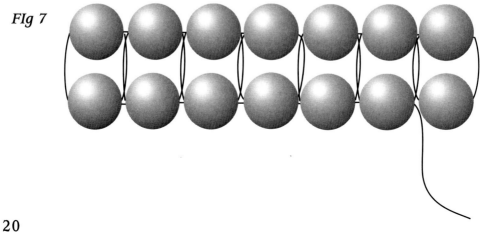

Section 3

Row 32 To Increase (fig 8)

Turn the work, stitch the 7 beads below the final 7 of section 2 and then pick up 5 beads plus the first bead of the next row (row 33) which is stitched exactly as for the first bead in Row 2 (fig 1). Work into all the beads and finish the row.

At 'Z' pick up 5 more beads *plus the first bead from the row above* and work back until you meet the end of the previous row bead 'X'. Remember to take your stabilizing thread through the row just stitched and the previous row at the end of every second row of stitching. You are now ready to begin row 34.

On completion of the design finish your thread in the usual way.

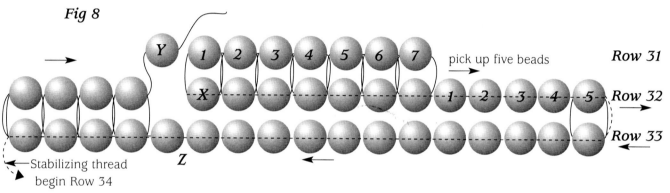

Fig 8

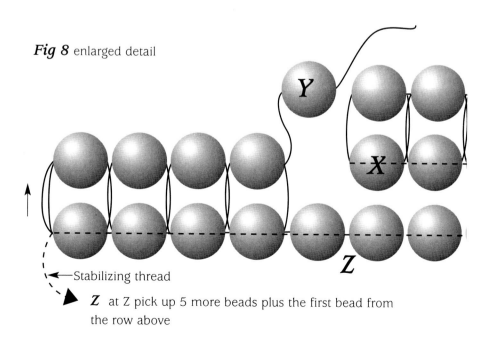

Fig 8 enlarged detail

Z at Z pick up 5 more beads plus the first bead from the row above

The Fringe

This very simple fringe reminds me of a piu piu, from traditional Maori skirts. The fringe strands increase in length to the centre and then decrease again. There is one strand for every bead across the bottom of the book mark.

Cut and wax a 1.5m (5ft) length of thread. Weave through the main body of work, working several clove hitches to secure the thread and bring the needle out from the bottom left bead. Starting at the left hand side pick up three black beads and work following the chart. Use the last bead as a turning bead and go back through all the beads to the top, re-entering the bead from the opposite side so it hangs evenly (fig 9). Take your thread through the bead above and the one to its right and come out of the next bead along the bottom row. Do this at the top of each strand and complete the fringe following the chart. Fasten off your thread in the main body of work in the usual manner. Now all you need is an excellent book to put your masterpiece to good work!

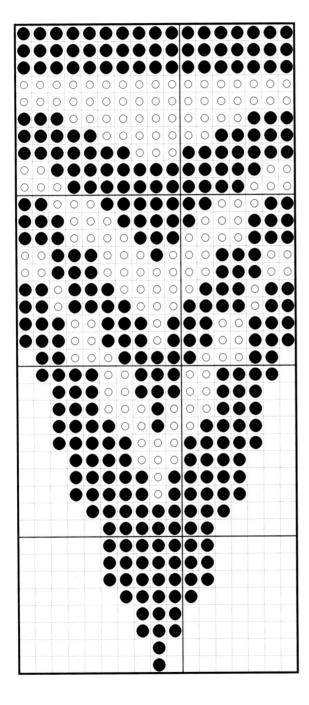

Fig 9

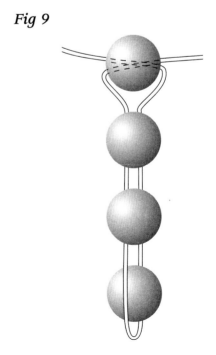

Key

●	black
○	silver

Turquoise Collar

refer to colour photograph page 38

Beads were used as an item of exchange in trade more than 2000 years ago. Their decorative qualities were appreciated even earlier and beaded collars and necklaces have adorned necks from earliest times. The inspiration for this design comes from tribal art. The net symbolises an earlier way of life, living predominantly on fish from the bounty of the ocean, when bones and shells were used for tools and adornment. Early beads were hand drilled and threaded on horsehair. Today beads are purchased ready drilled, with needles and threads designed especially for use with them.

Netting weave is extremely simple and versatile and has the advantage that it molds well to enhance every body shape. This neck collar is made mainly using bugle and seed beads with some heishe and triangular beads for added interest, if you preferred these could be replaced with seed beads. It is a very beautiful piece of jewellery that will not fail to attract attention.

Materials.

- 7g turquoise bugles approx 1.2cm (1/2") in length
- 8g turquoise seed beads
- 8g size 8 Jade beads
- 1g silver seed beads
- 1g heishe turquoise tubular beads 2mm (1/8" approx.) in length*
- 5g jade triangular beads 2mm (1/8" approx.) in length*
- 1 x magnetic silver clasp
- Nymo® thread to match
- Beading needle
- Wax

*these beads could be replaced with seed beads

Note: Magnetic clasps should not be used by those wearing a pacemaker.

Technique: Netting

Instructions

This necklace can be adjusted to fit any neck by altering the length of the foundation row. The technique and instructions remain the same regardless of the number of beads in the foundation row.

Row 1 Foundation Row Cut and wax a 1.5m (5ft) length of thread. Tie on a keeper bead 20cm (8") from the end of the thread. A keeper bead is tied on with a simple half knot *that can be undone easily later,* to prevent the other beads from slipping off the thread. Pick up a size 8 jade bead then add a bugle, continue picking up the two beads alternately, until you have 28 size 8 jade beads and 27 bugles, ending with a Size 8 jade bead (fig 1). To adjust the length add or remove beads at this point until it fits your neck comfortably. Finish with a size 8 jade bead.

Pick up the clasp and attach securely, then take the needle back through all the beads working two or three clove hitches between the first few beads to secure the clasp. Once back at the beginning remove the keeper bead, pick up the other half of the clasp and attach securely. (For detailed information on attaching a clasp see page 8.) Continue working with the long end of thread. Fasten off the shorter end of thread in the usual way (for finishing threads see page 8).

Fig 1

Row 2 Go through the first size 8 jade bead in the foundation row and pick up six turquoise seed beads, one size 8 jade bead and six more seed beads then take your needle through the next size 8 jade bead (fig. 2). Continue doing this to the end of the row. Work a clove hitch between the first bead and catch on the first row. This secures this row of stitching and allows you to turn. Without the knot the netting could become too loose.

Now go back down the six seed beads and through the jade bead. The size 8 jade beads are the connecting beads on each row.

Fig 2

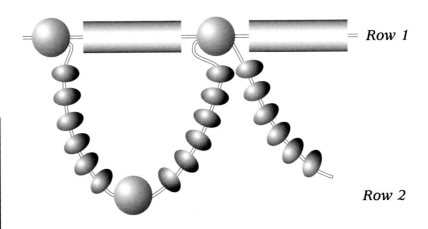

Row 1

Row 2

HANDY HINT

Use this technique to fringe the edge of a scarf, cuffs or hems!

Row 3 Pick up one bugle, one size 8 jade bead and another bugle and go through the jade bead on the second row (fig. 3). Continue in this way to the end of the row. When you reach the end of the row, go all the way up the seed beads to the first row. Go through the bugle and back down the seed beads at the other side of it, back through the bugle in the third row and the jade bead to reach the correct position for starting Row 4.

Row 4 (not illustrated) Pick up a turquoise heishe bead, two jade triangular beads, a heishe, a size 8 jade bead, a heishe, two jade triangular and another heishe bead. Go through the jade bead at the centre of the bugles on row three.

Repeat this combination of beads until the end of this row. To get your needle in the correct position to start the final row, take the needle through the jade bead and work your way around the diamond of bugle, seed beads, jade bead, seed beads and bugle and then back down through the heishe and triangular beads ready to start your final row.

Fig 3

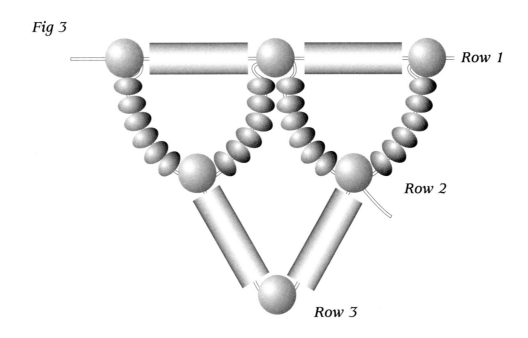

Row 1

Row 2

Row 3

Fig 4

Row 5 As this is the final row of the necklace I added a silver seed bead to enhance and highlight the tip of each section. Pick up eight turquoise seed beads, a size 8 jade bead, a turquoise heishe bead and a silver seed bead. The silver seed bead is the turning bead. Bring your thread around the silver bead and go back through the heishe and size 8 jade beads. Pull the thread gently into place to form a little point then pick up eight more turquoise seed beads before going through the jade bead at the centre of the first section of the previous row. Continue in this way to the end of the row. Fasten your thread off securely in the usual way.

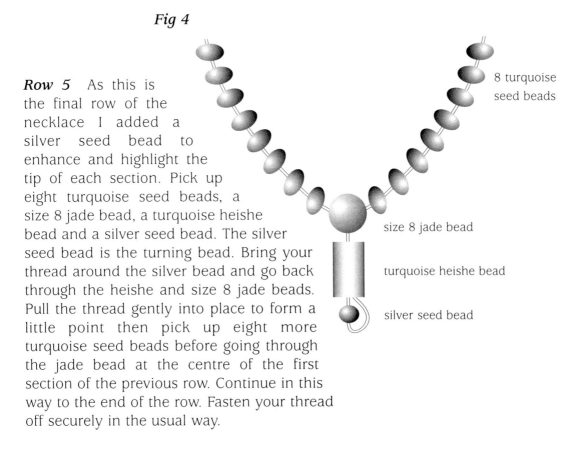

8 turquoise seed beads

size 8 jade bead

turquoise heishe bead

silver seed bead

This technique is most effective and you can continue for as many rows as you wish, making the collar much longer if desired. It is particularly stunning with a narrow strap or strapless dress as the fluidity of the collar means it sits well.

Evening Moth

refer to the colour photograph page 42

This elegant amulet purse introduces a new technique, tubular peyote stitch. Instead of the beads lying flat they appear 'end on' in the finished design. It is worked over a cardboard tube and it is important to get the tension correct from the beginning. The subtly contrasting colours show the moth hovering in the darkening sky as the sun goes down, throwing out resplendent pinks and mauves with just a touch of the daylight within.

Materials

- 15g blue antique seed beads Mill Hill 03061 referred to as main colour
- 9g rose pink seed beads Mill Hill 00553
- 5g purple antique seed beads Mill Hill 03034
- 4.5g pale blue seed beads Mill Hill 00143
- 3g pink small bugle beads Mill Hill 72051
- An assortment of decorative matching beads for the necklace strap and for use in the fringe lengths
- 36 decorative beads/drops for fringe ends
- Nymo® thread to match
- Wax
- Two beading needles
- Lightweight card

Technique: Tubular Even Count Peyote Stitch

Instructions

The patterned border at the base of this design makes it an easy way to learn tubular even count peyote stitch.

Rows 1 & 2 Cut and wax a 1.5m (5ft) length of thread. Pick up pink, purple, pink and light blue beads in this four bead sequence until you have 68 beads and tie into a circle 50cms (20") from the end of the thread (fig 1). When tying the circle allow enough room for about two extra beads. This space will be used in the third row.

NOTE The 68 beads you have already threaded will become the first and second row.

Take a piece of lightweight card and roll into a tube to snugly fit your circle and tape to size. I roll the card up tightly then allow it to expand within the circle of beads to get the size right. Only then do I tape it in place. Position the circle of beads near the top of the tube so that you can hold the thread tightly between your fingers inside the roll with your thumb on top of the roll.

> **HANDY HINT**
>
> Make sure the Cylinder is the same size top and bottom.

26

Fig 1

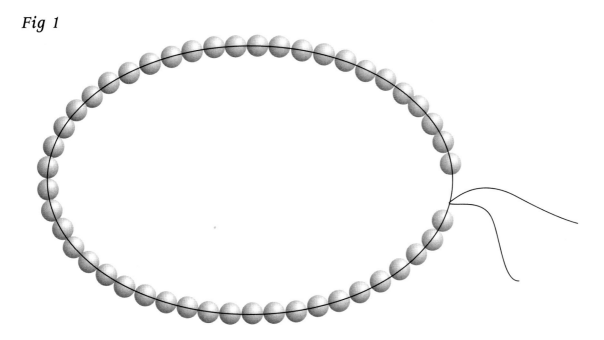

Row 3 Working from ***right to left and up*** the cylinder, thread the needle through the first bead to the left of the knot, in this case the first pink bead you threaded. Pick up a purple bead, miss a bead and go through the third bead from the knot another pink bead, (fig 2). As you pull the thread taut it pushes down the neighbouring bead thus forming two rows (fig. 3).

Fig 2

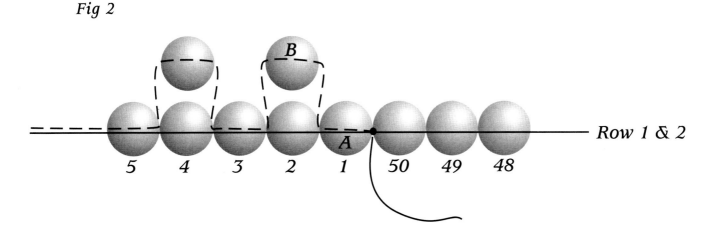

Continue around the circle picking up a light blue or a purple bead alternately and always stitching through the pink beads until you get to the end of the row, bead Z (fig 4). You will see the pattern forming as you do this.

Fig 3

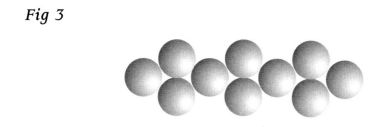

Row 4 is worked in pink. To continue into the fourth row you must 'step up'. Take the needle back through the first bead, bead A, then stitch through the first bead of row 3, bead B. This forms the 'Step', now pick up the first bead for the next row (a pink bead) and you are ready to continue row 4 (fig. 4). You will move up the rows in this diagonal manner each time. The pink beads line up with the earlier pink beads see photograph page 42 so it is easy to check you are stitching correctly.

At the end of each row - always remember pick up the last bead of the row, then take the needle through the first bead of the previous row then through the first bead you picked up in this row and then pick up a new bead to continue the new row - refer to fig. 4 if you feel uncertain.

Care is needed in following the chart but you will find it easier if you follow the design and ignore the plain beads. Each row starts one bead to the left of the previous row. When you have completed all the rows in the diagram finish your thread in the usual way.

Remove the work from the tube, centre the design, press flat and over sew the bottom edge of the purse with the thread end left at the beginning. Finish off the thread as before.

Fig 4

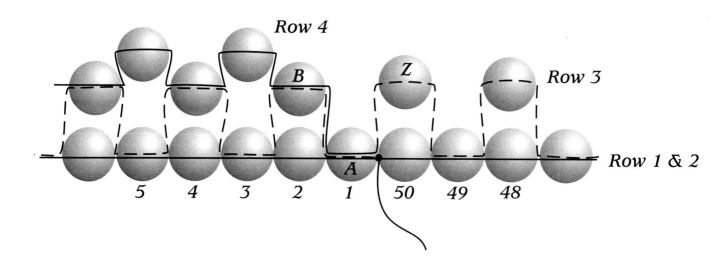

Following the Chart

In this chart you work from the bottom of the purse up and from the bottom of the chart up. The arrow shows the starting point. The initial 68 beads picked up become rows 1 & 2, each row is 34 beads long. On the chart the pattern starts at row 13, row 4 is marked with a dot.

Key

○ blue antique seed beads (main colour)

● purple

● blue

● pink

Fringe

A luxuriant fringe is extremely attractive but before you start beading work out how you want your strands of fringe to look. Often a strand of fringe is added to every bead across the base of the purse, the more strands there are the more luxuriant the fringe. If the individual strands are going to vary, lay the different strands on your felt until you have a pleasing arrangement. I have three different patterns in this fringing and it is stitched onto alternate beads front and back.

Cut and wax a 1.5m (5ft) length of thread and secure into the main body of the purse, emerging from the purple bead at the bottom right hand edge. On completion of the first strand stitch through the same purple bead from the other side to ensure that the strand will hang evenly (fig 5). Take your thread to the next bead in the base of the purse, in this case a blue bead and work the next strand of the fringe, continue in this manner until the fringe is completed.

Strand 3 *These strands come from every pink bead across the back of the purse. Each strand is identical in format, except for the feature beads at the base of the strands which vary.*

Strand 1 *This is the fringe for each purple bead across the front of the purse.*

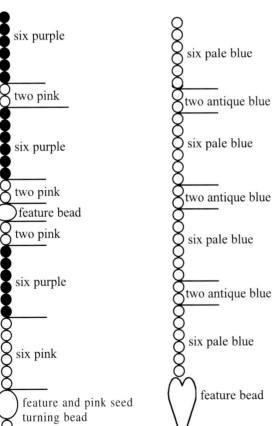

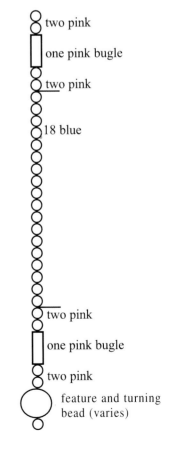

two pink
one pink bugle
two pink

18 blue

two pink
one pink bugle
two pink
feature and turning bead (varies)

Strand 2 *This is the fringe for each blue bead across the front of the purse. I have used little silver leaves at the end of these strands so no turning bead is necessary.*

30

Fig 5

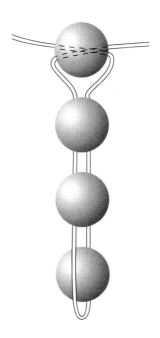

Neck Strap *(68cm)*

Before you start sort out your feature beads and arrange in the order in which they will appear. Remember, you only have to design half the length required as the second half will be a mirror image of the first.

Cut and wax two, 1m (1 1/4yd) lengths of thread. As the neck strap only measures 68cms (27") slightly shorter lengths of thread can be used. Thread each length onto beading needles and secure in the main body of work before bringing your needles out at the left hand edge, on the top row. Bring one thread out from each side of a bead and pick up a pink bead. I prefer to work from one side using two needles rather than taking one very long thread from one side to the other then back, as it is easy to split the thread on the way back resulting in awkward tangles. This is my personal preference, do it which ever way you prefer.

With needle one pick up 20 more pink beads to start the neck strap, then continue picking up a pleasing arrangement of beads using the beads in the purse design plus any feature beads you wish to add, until you have reached the midpoint. Now reverse the arrangement until you are back to the final 21 pink seed beads. With the second needle I worked peyote stitch into the 21 beads at the start of the neck strap on each side, and have worked odd areas of peyote stitch throughout the neck strap. I have also put a second line of beads beside the first returning to a single strand after a varying number of beads in different places. Have some fun and just fiddle! Beading is a relaxing and enjoyable occupation, so enjoy! Refer to the colour photograph page 42 for additional detail.

Secure the thread on the opposite side of the bag down in the main body of the purse taking the thread through the beads and working two or three clove hitches in the usual way. Now wear your necklace and enjoy it!

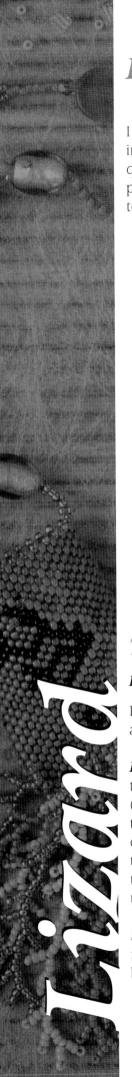

Lizard in the Grass

refer to the colour photograph page 40

I have long been interested in brightly coloured frogs and amphibians and often incorporate them into my art designs. This colourful little lizard weaves its way quickly across the lawn after emerging from the tangled undergrowth. This project is fun to make, the rich heavy fringe enhancing the design and adding to the story.

Materials

- 2g bright orange seed beads Mill Hill 02060
- 2g black seed beads Mill Hill 02014
- two yellow beads for eyes, plus extra for use in fringe, optional
- 14g green seed beads Mill Hill 02067
- 9g frosted green seed beads Mill Hill 62049
- 9g iridescent green seed beads Mill Hill 00167
- 4.5g light green seed beads Mill Hill 02066 *fringe only*
- 6x1cm (1/2") oval green feature beads for *neck strap*
- 6x1cm (1/2") round green feature beads for *neck strap*
- 4x6mm (1/4") crystal beads for *neck strap*
- 12x3mm (1/8") cut crystal beads for *neck strap*
- Nymo® thread to match
- Two beading needles
- wax
- Lightweight card

Technique: Tubular Even Count Peyote Stitch

Instructions

I have worked this little bag from the lizard's tail up finishing the top edge with alternate plain and iridescent green beads forming a crenellated edge.

Rows 1 & 2 Cut and wax a 1.5m (5ft) length of thread. Pick up 50 green beads, the main colour, and tie into a circle 50cms (20") from the end of the thread (fig. 1). Do not pull too tightly but allow enough room for two more beads in the circle. Take a piece of lightweight card and roll into a tube to snugly fit your circle and tape to size. I roll the card up tightly then allow it to expand within the circle of beads to get the size right. Only then do I tape it in place. Position the circle of beads near the top of the tube so that you can hold the thread tightly between your fingers inside the roll and thumb on top of the roll.

NOTE This circle of 50 beads becomes rows 1 & 2 when you add the third row of beads. The pattern starts on row 4.

HANDY HINT

Make sure the Cylinder is the same size top and bottom.

Fig 1

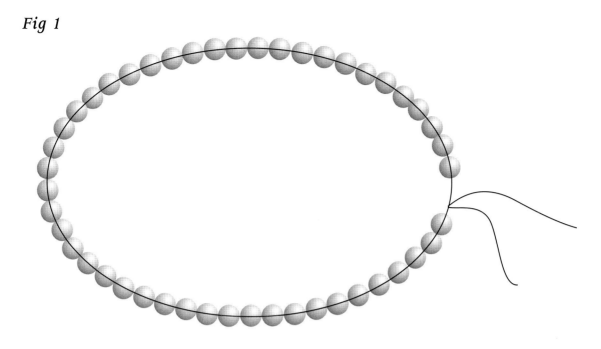

Row 3 Working from ***right to left and up the cylinder,*** using the same green beads, take the needle through the first bead to the left of the knot. Pick up a bead, miss a bead and go through the third bead to the left of the knot (fig. 2).

Fig 2

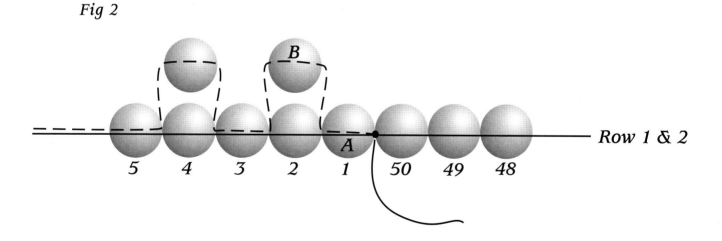

As you pull the thread taut it pushes down the neighbouring bead thus forming two rows (fig. 3). Pick up another bead, miss a bead and go through the next bead. Continue in this manner until you reach the end of the row, bead Z (fig 4).

Fig 3

Row 4 To move into the next row you must make a 'step up'. Take the needle back through bead A on the diagram, then stitch through the first bead of row three, bead B. This forms the step, (fig. 4). You are now ready to continue with the fourth row.

Each row begins one bead to the left of the previous row. Refer back to fig 4 at the end of each row to ensure that you follow the correct sequence when moving onto the next row. *Pick up the last bead of the row, then take the needle through the first bead of the previous row then through the first bead you picked up in this row and then pick up a new bead to continue the new row.*

Fig 4

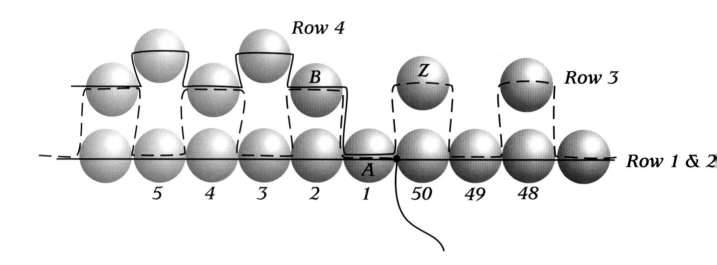

The pattern starts in row 4, work 12 main colour beads pick up one black bead then the rest of the work is worked in green. Follow the chart carefully until all the rows have been completed.

The lizards eyes are larger than the seed beads but just add them in the usual way. The third to last and last rows are worked in iridescent green beads while the second to last row is worked in plain green. This adds interest to the crenellated top edge of the little purse.

On completion of the beading, centre the design, flatten the purse edges together and oversew the bottom edge. You can now begin the fringe.

HANDY HINT

Practice this technique using a smaller number of bigger beads, with each row a different colour.

Following the Chart

Follow this chart by working from the bottom of the chart up. You are working from the base of the purse to the top.

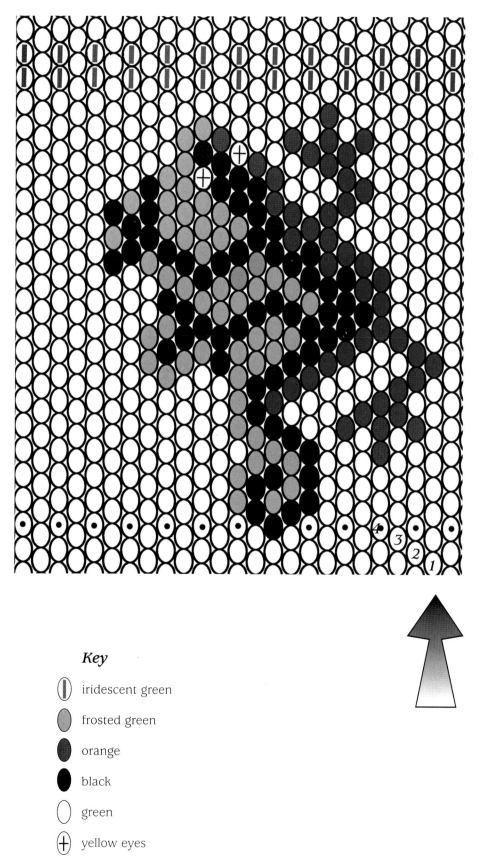

Key

🗍 iridescent green

🔘 frosted green

⬤ orange

⬤ black

◯ green

⊕ yellow eyes

35

Fig 5

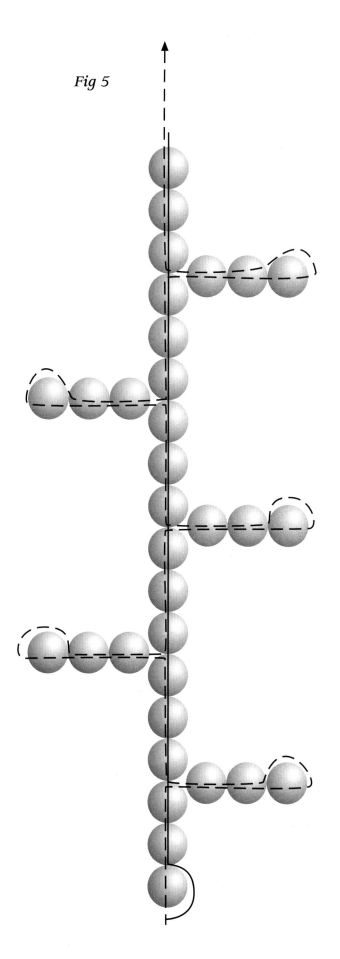

Fringe

Cut and wax a 1.5m (5ft) length of thread. Fasten the end securely into the purse at the back, weaving through several beads and working two or three clove hitches. Emerge from the first bead on the bottom edge, at the left hand side of the purse.

Pick up 30 green beads, turn on the thirtieth and go back through two beads. Then pick up three more beads, which will stick out at the side forming a little 'shoot'. Turn on the third bead, going back through the other two to the main strand, then go up three more beads on the main strand. Pick up three more beads and work in the same manner all the way back up to the top of the strand to the edge of the purse (fig 5). When creating a fringe come out one side of a bead and return on the other side to ensure that the fringe strands will hang evenly. Take your thread back up through two or three beads in the body of the bag before emerging from the next bead along the base of the purse ready to make the next strand of the fringe.

Work your way across the base of the bag making the strands of the fringe the same way each time but increasing the length of each strand by three beads until you have 48 beads. Six beads from the right hand side of the bag start decreasing by three beads for each strand of the fringe. Alternate the beads for the fringe using, iridescent green beads, frosted green, light green and green. There are 22 strands to my fringe in total.

For interest add more yellow eye beads at the end of the offshoots randomly through the fringe to give the illusion of more lizards peeping out of the grass!

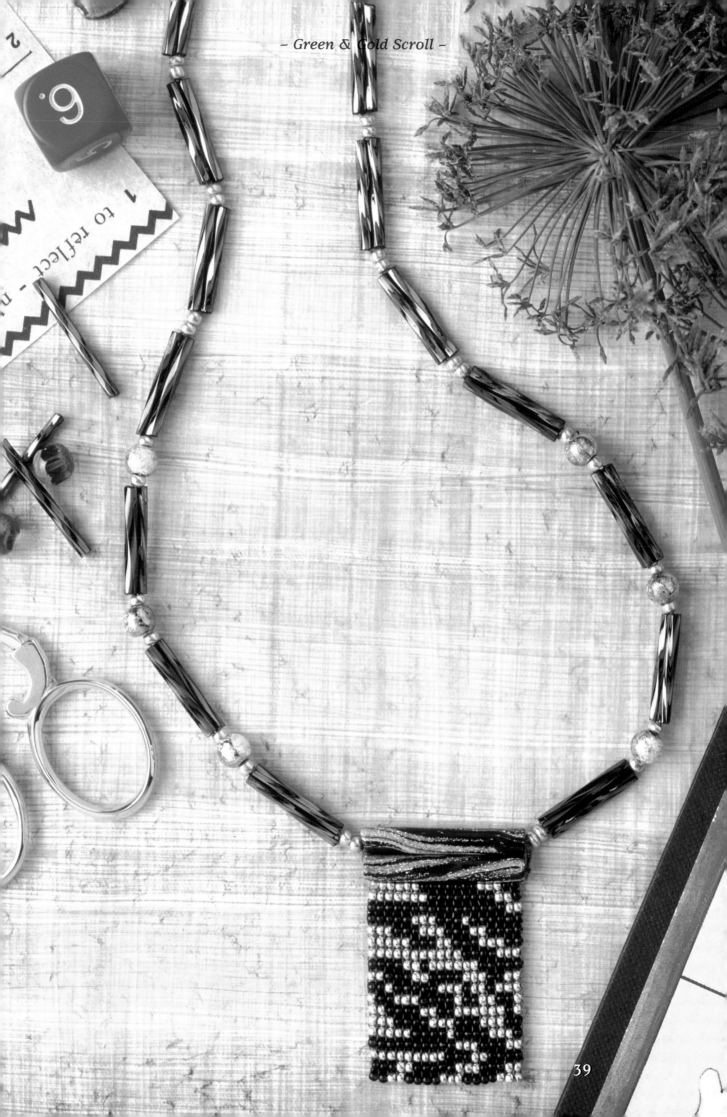

~ Sunstone Pendant ~

lapis lazuli - ḥsbd

– *Snowflake Bracelet & Necklace* –

Neck strap

Cut and wax two lengths of thread each approximately 1m (1yd) in length. Secure the threads in the main body of the purse in the usual way and bring your needles out at the left hand edge, on the top row. Bring one thread out from each side of a bead and pick up an iridescent bead, threading both needles through it from opposite sides and pull firmly into position.

I prefer to work from one side using two needles rather than taking one very long thread from one side to the other then back, as it is easy to split the thread on the way back resulting in disastrous tangles. Do it which ever way you personally prefer. Make the neckstrap following this diagram or create your own design. When a sufficient length has been created for the neckstrap, separate the threads and take them through a bead at the top right hand edge of the purse. Take one thread through the bead from each side as this will ensure the neckstrap hangs nicely. Finish the thread ends in the body of the purse in the usual way.

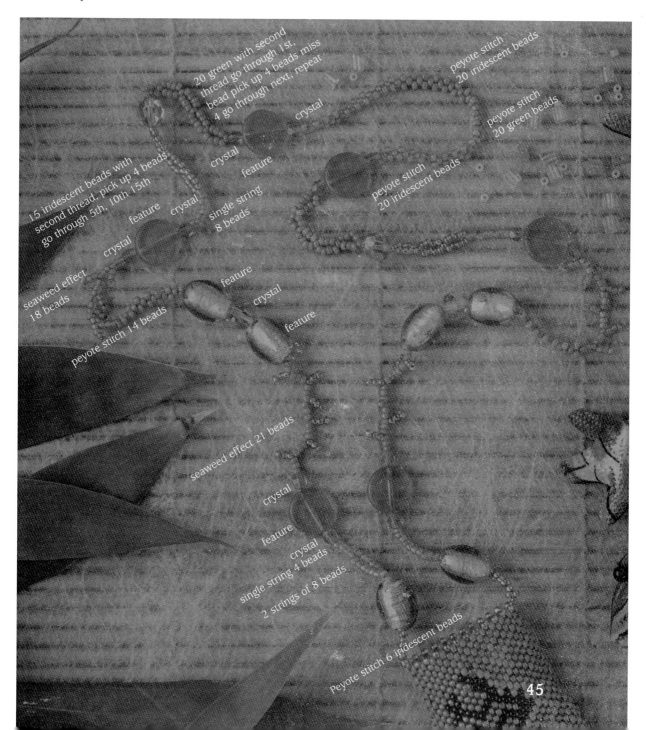

Beads of Time Necklace

refer to the colour photograph page 43

I have always been interested in other cultures and find it fascinating that we can still learn so much from methods employed by earlier peoples. Ancient Egyptian beads were threaded and woven on horsehair using similar techniques to those used in making these designs. The Egyptians had a love of beautifully crafted artifacts often using gold from Nubia, or lower Egypt. This neckpiece and earrings were inspired by the ornate bejewelled collars worn by ancient Egyptian nobility. The green, red and blue seed beads were chosen to represent emeralds, rubies and sapphires thus giving an illusion of wealth to this intricate piece of jewellery.

Materials

- 15g gold seed beads Mill Hill 00557
- 9g green seed beads Mill Hill 02020
- 9g blue seed beads Mill Hill 00020
- 9g red seed beads Mill Hill 03049
- Nymo® thread to match
- Wax
- 2 x beading needles
- 1 x magnetic gold clasp.

Important: The magnetic gold clasp is not suitable for people wearing a pacemaker.

Technique: Honeycomb and Brick stitch

The 'rope' is stitched in honeycomb technique which is easy to do and produces an attractive tubular effect. The centrepiece is worked in brick stitch.

Rope Necklace

The necklace is made in two parts. First a simple but very elegant 'bejewelled' rope necklace which can be proudly worn alone. If you wish to make a bolder 'statement' add the centrepiece!

First circle

Cut and wax a 1.5m length of thread. Wax well and repeat frequently whilst beading. Pick up six gold beads, go back through the first bead (A) to make a circle. Leave a 30cm (12") length of thread at the beginning to attach the clasp (fig 1).

Fig 1

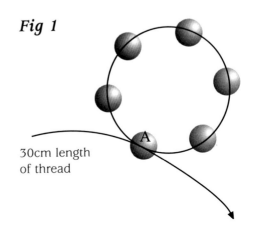

30cm length
of thread

Second circle (dashed line)

Keep the 30cm (12") length of thread firmly wrapped around the fingers of your left hand. * Pick up three beads (one gold, one red and one gold) miss a bead and go through the next*. Repeat twice. Keep the beads firmly between the thumb and first finger of your left hand so that you do not change direction by mistake (fig 2).

Fig 2

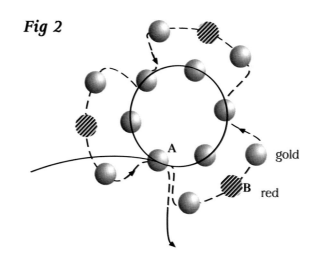

gold

B red

Third circle

Continue picking up three beads, but in this row pick up one gold one blue and one gold and go through the red beads in the previous row (fig. 3). *You will go through the contrast bead B next but one from where your thread is for the first stitch but for the next three stitches there are three gold beads between the contrast beads.*

Before continuing any further, pull the 30cm (12") length firmly from the left and the thread from the right. The beads will, with a little encouragement, form a little "vessel" in appearance, with the beads coming forward to form a hollow tube, which is closed at the base. This is where the clasp will be attached later. Continue to work in this tubular form for the rest of your stitching. Keep the tension on the thread to ensure that the correct shape develops.

Fig 3

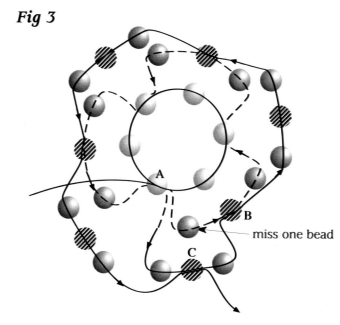

miss one bead

Forth circle (dotted line)

As before, pick up three beads. In this row pick up one gold one green and one gold. Go through the blue bead in the previous row. Repeat twice more to complete the row (fig. 4).

Continue beading changing the contrast bead each row from red to blue to green back to red, until the piece measures 40cms (16"), or fits your neck comfortably.

Fig 4

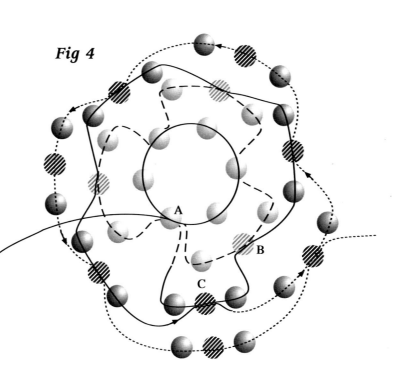

Changing Threads

You will have to use about three lengths of thread to reach the desired length. Stop sewing when you have about 20cms (8") of thread left. Cut a new 1.5m (5ft) length of thread and wax well. With another needle weave your thread through the tube working three clove hitches on the way. Emerge in exactly the same position as your previous thread and continue beading with this new piece of thread ensuring that you have not changed direction. Once you have worked a couple of centimetres (one inch) using the new length of thread you can weave the old short length in and fasten off in the usual way.

To finish

Take your needle through the last three contrast beads to draw in the 'tube' before attaching the clasp. Attach clasp firmly and weave your thread ends back through the beadwork working several clove hitches to secure the thread end. Return to the starting point of your necklace and attach the clasp there also. I used a magnetic clasp with a 'tubular' appearance which fits in well with the tubular shape of the rope necklace.

Centre Piece

The centre piece is worked in brick stitch. It has a straight top edge and the design is started here. Read all the instructions before you begin!

Row 1 Foundation row.

Cut and wax a 1.5m (5ft) length of thread and thread both ends with beading needles. Pick up a gold bead and position it about 30cms (12") from one end of your thread (fig.5). Pick up a second gold bead and thread a needle through from each side, drawing it in next to the first bead (fig. 6). Repeat with a third bead (fig.7).

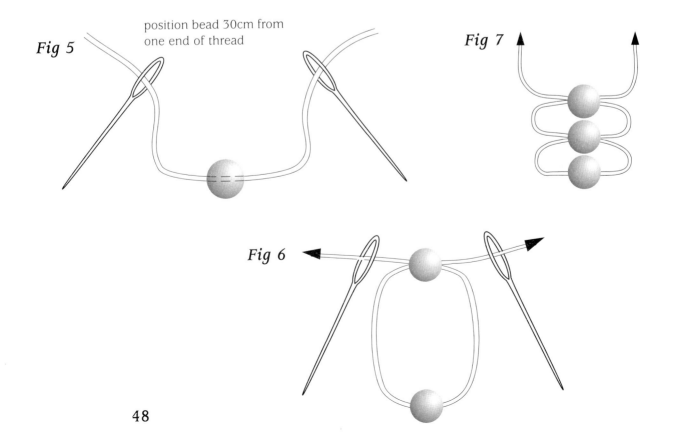

Fig 5

position bead 30cm from one end of thread

Fig 7

Fig 6

Continue until you have 30 gold beads threaded, these form your foundation row. At the end of the row take each needle back through the second to last bead and then out through the last bead again (fig 8). This secures the end bead and makes it easier to start working Row 2.

Fig 8

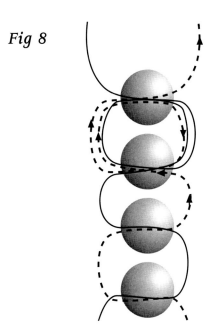

Row 2 Holding your beads with the two threads to the right hand side pick up the needle attached to the longer thread and turn your beads to make sure this thread is coming out of the top of the end bead. Pick up one gold bead and, stitching towards yourself, bring the needle under the thread between the first and second bead of the previous row and then back up through the gold bead (fig 9). You are now on the second row of the chart. Pick up another gold bead and repeat the process, under the thread between the next two beads and back up through the bead you picked up. Continue in this manner until you reach the end of the row – there are 29 beads in this row and the last bead is joined by taking the needle under the thread between the last two beads in the previous row.

Fig 9 to start picking up one bead

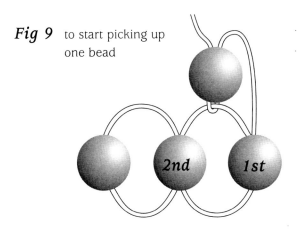

Rows 3, 5 & 7 Following the chart, pick up two gold beads and stitch under the thread between the first and second bead of the previous row. Go back up through the second bead only (fig 10), being careful to ensure that the first bead lies correctly when the stitch is completed.

Fig 10
picking up two beads

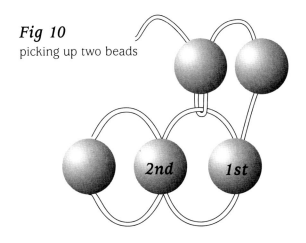

Following The Chart

Start at the bottom of this chart and work up. Arrows show the starting point and direction in which the rows are stitched. For easy reference the rows are numbered.

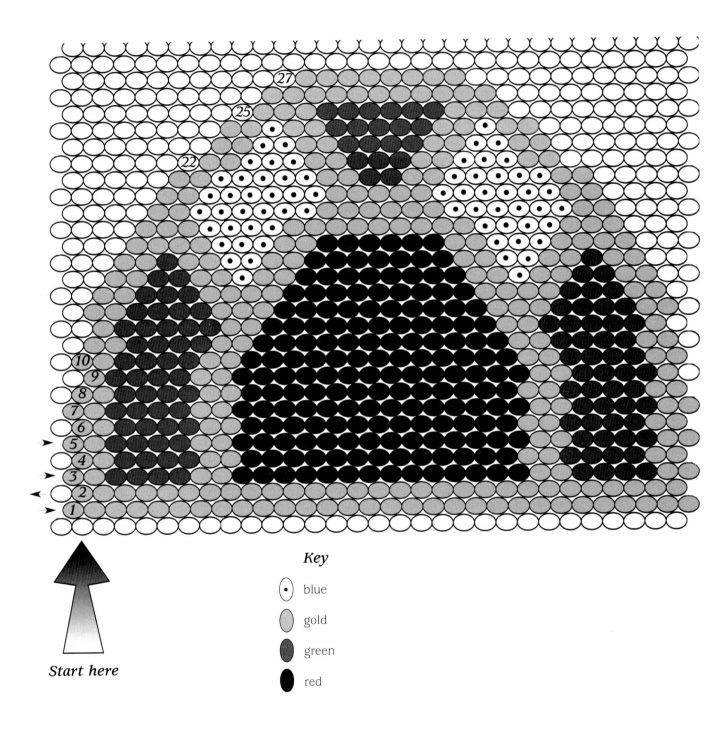

Start here

Key

- (•) blue
- ◯ gold
- ◯ green
- ● red

At the end of the row attach the last bead by stitching under the thread at the end of the previous row (fig.11). This ensures that the bead 'juts out' at the end of the row as it does at the beginning.

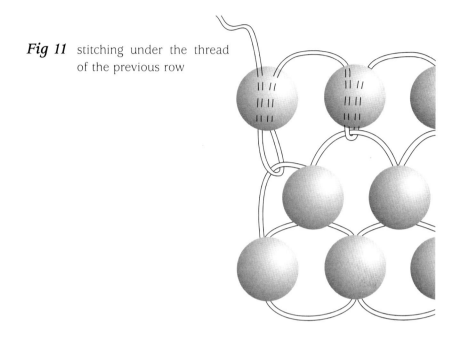

Fig 11 stitching under the thread of the previous row

Rows 4, 6 & 8 Pick up one gold bead and, stitching towards yourself, bring the needle under the thread between the first and second bead of the previous row and then back up through the gold bead (fig 9). Continue in this manner until you reach the end of the row – there are 29 beads in this row. Finish by taking the needle under the thread between the last two beads in the previous row.

Rows 9 - 27 Continue following the chart carefully. At all times careful attention must be paid to the colours of the beads you are working with to ensure the pattern remains correct. You may find it useful to use a ruler to mark the row you are working on.

HANDY HINT

To start, if the line on the chart goes in, pick up one bead, if the line 'juts out' pick up two. When finishing if the line 'juts out' finish as shown in fig 11, if the line goes in the last stitch is between the last two beads of the previous row.

Decreasing

From Row 13 onwards each row decreases to form the semi circular shape. In most rows you will decrease by just picking up one bead at the start of the row and finish the row by taking your needle under the thread between the last two beads of the previous row.

Rows 22, 25 and 27 marked on the chart, are worked differently. Instead of the needle being taken under the thread between the first two beads of the previous row it is taken under the thread between the second and third beads of the previous row. To get the thread into the correct position to start stitching row 22 for example, at the end of row 21 take the needle back down around the last bead into the row beneath across and up, before picking up a bead ready to continue (fig 12). It is important to take the thread down and round like this as it gives a very strong 'firm' edge.

To finish the Centre Piece: weave the thread back through the main body of work working two or three clove hitches before cutting the thread end off.

Fig 12 shaded thread shows thread path at end of row 21 to get to correct position to start Row 22

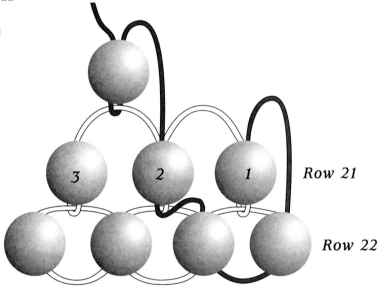

Row 21

Row 22

To create the loops: Return to the foundation row and thread your needle into the 30cm (12") thread length then take the needle and thread back along the work emerging from the seventh bead. Pick up a gold bead and stitching under the thread between the seventh and eighth beads join the bead as shown in fig 9. Join the second bead in the same way. Turn and working two beads in each row attach the first bead as in fig 9 and the second as in fig 11. This method of working ensures that the loop is very strong. There are 28 rows in total.

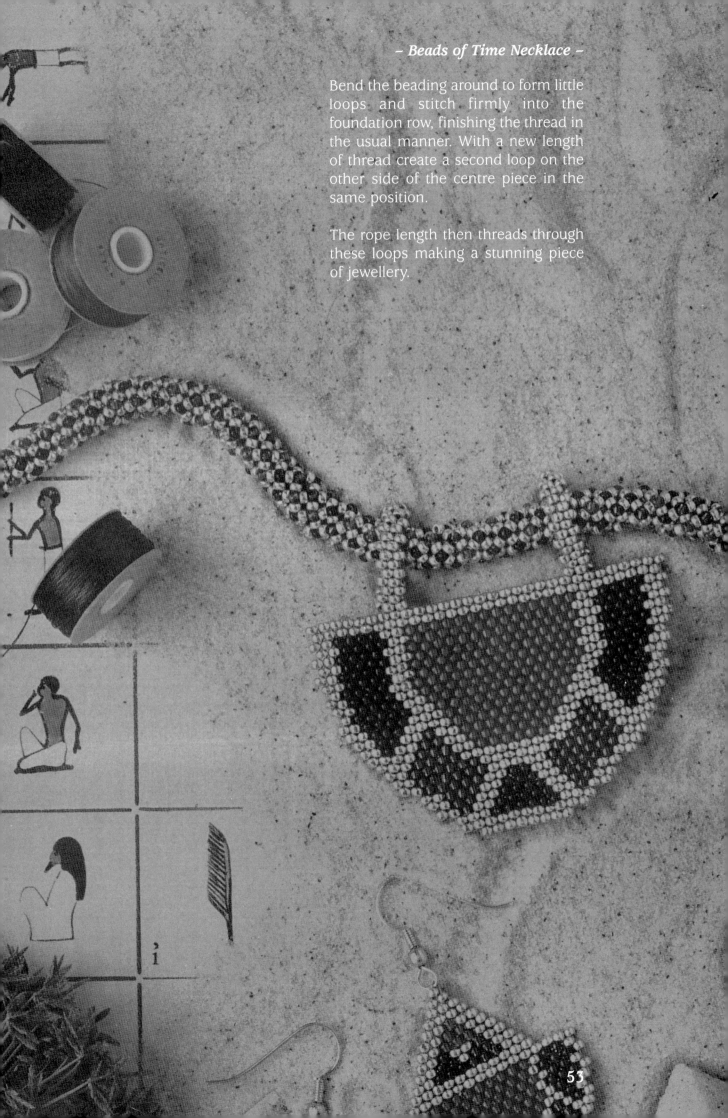

Bend the beading around to form little loops and stitch firmly into the foundation row, finishing the thread in the usual manner. With a new length of thread create a second loop on the other side of the centre piece in the same position.

The rope length then threads through these loops making a stunning piece of jewellery.

Beads of Time Earrings

refer to the colour photograph page 43

Having made the necklace, why not complete the set with these exuberant matching earrings?

Materials

- 5g gold seed beads Mill Hill 00557
- 2g red seed beads Mill Hill 03049
- 1g blue seed beads Mill Hill 00020
- 1g green seed beads Mill Hill 02020
- 1 pair French ear wires, gold
- Nymo® thread to match
- wax
- two beading needles.

Technique: Brick stitch

Instructions.

The earrings are made with the same techniques used in making the centre piece of the Beads of Time Necklace. They are started at the widest point, the straight row of gold beads - 18 beads wide and then worked up and down from this point. Read all the instructions before commencing.

Rounded Section of Earring

Row 1 Foundation Row Cut and wax a 1.5m (5ft) length of thread. Thread both ends with a beading needle then pick up a gold bead and position it in the centre of your thread (fig1). Pick up a second gold bead and thread it from each side, drawing the bead down next to the first (fig 2). Repeat until you have 18 beads (fig 3). At the end of the row take each needle back through the second to last bead and then out through the last bead again (fig 4). This secures the end bead and makes it easier to start working Row 2

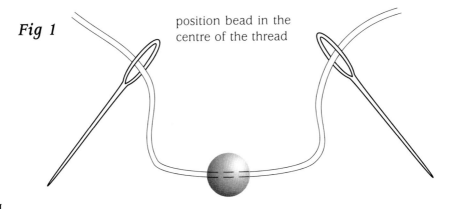

Fig 1

position bead in the centre of the thread

Fig 2

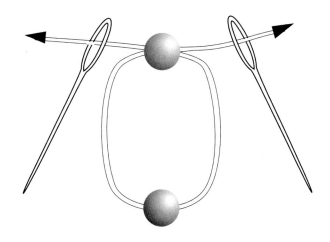

Fig 3

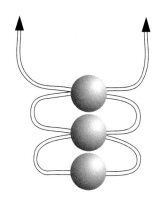

Fig 4

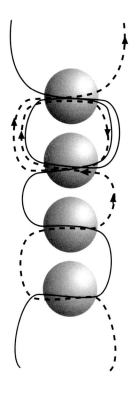

Row 2 Holding your beads with the two threads to the right hand side pick up the needle attached to the longer thread and turn your beads to make sure this thread is coming out of the top of the end bead. Pick up one gold bead. Stitching towards yourself, bring the needle under the thread between the first and second bead and then go back up through the gold bead which you have just picked up (fig 5). Continue in this way following the chart to the end of the row.

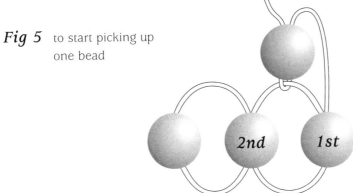

Fig 5 to start picking up
one bead

Row 3 Turn the work and this time, as the line in the chart *'juts out'*, pick up two beads, a gold and a green bead, stitch under the thread between the first and second bead then take your needle back up through the green bead only, making sure that the gold bead is positioned correctly (fig 6). At the end of the row, pick up the thread at the end of the previous row to add the last bead. (fig 7). This ensures that the bead 'juts out' at the end of the row as it does at the beginning.

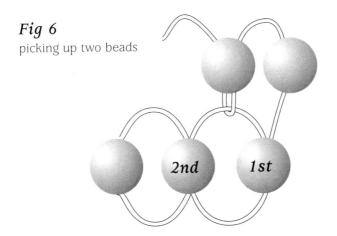

Fig 6
picking up two beads

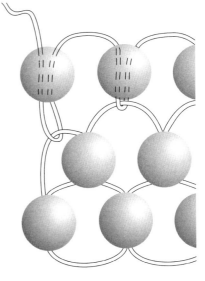

Fig 7 stitching under the
thread of the
previous row

HANDY HINT

To start, if the line on the chart goes in, pick up one bead, if the line 'juts out' pick up two. When finishing if the line 'juts out' finish as shown in fig 7 if the line goes in the last stitch is between the last two beads of the previous row.

Following the Chart

This chart is started at Row 1 which is the widest point. Bead upwards from here to form the curved section. Follow the chart on page 59 to work rows A-K.

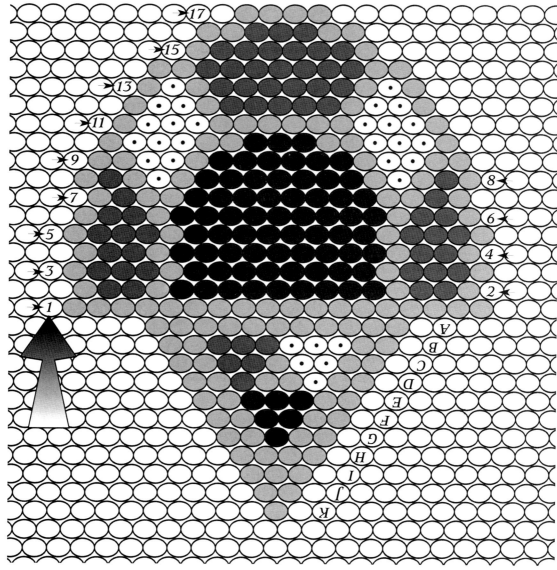

Start here for curved area

Key

⊙	blue
⬤	gold
⬤	green
⬤	red

Continue to follow the chart until the end decreasing as required to form the rounded lower edge. In most rows you will decrease by just picking up one bead at the start of the row and finish the row by taking your needle under the thread of the last two beads of the previous row.

Row 15 and 17 are worked differently. Instead of the needle being taken under the thread between the first two beads of the previous row it is taken under the thread between the second and third beads of the previous row. To get the thread into the correct position to start take the needle back down around the last bead into the row beneath across and up, before picking up a bead ready to continue (fig 8). It is important to take the thread down and round like this as it gives a very strong 'firm' edge.

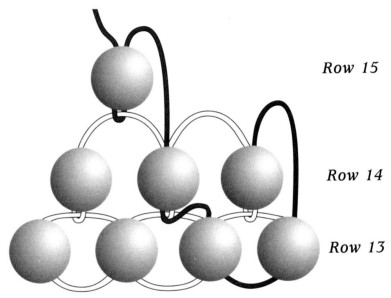

Fig 8 shaded thread shows thread path at end of row 14 to get to correct position to start Row 15

Row 15

Row 14

Row 13

To make the point

Return to the starting point, and weave the other end of thread back through the work to emerge from the fourth bead ready to begin Row A. Pick up a gold bead and bring your needle under the thread between the fourth and fifth beads and then go back up through the bead (fig 5). Join 11 gold beads in this row.

Following the Chart

Follow the chart to form the top half of the earring. The decrease is accomplished by picking up one bead only at the start of the row and by taking the needle under the thread between the last two beads of the previous row to finish the row. When you reach the final bead stitch firmly around the French ear wire taking several stitches and weaving the thread through several rows of beads for strength. Finish the thread in the usual way.

Repeat for the second earring. They are not heavy to wear and the jewel coloured beads reflect the light beautifully.

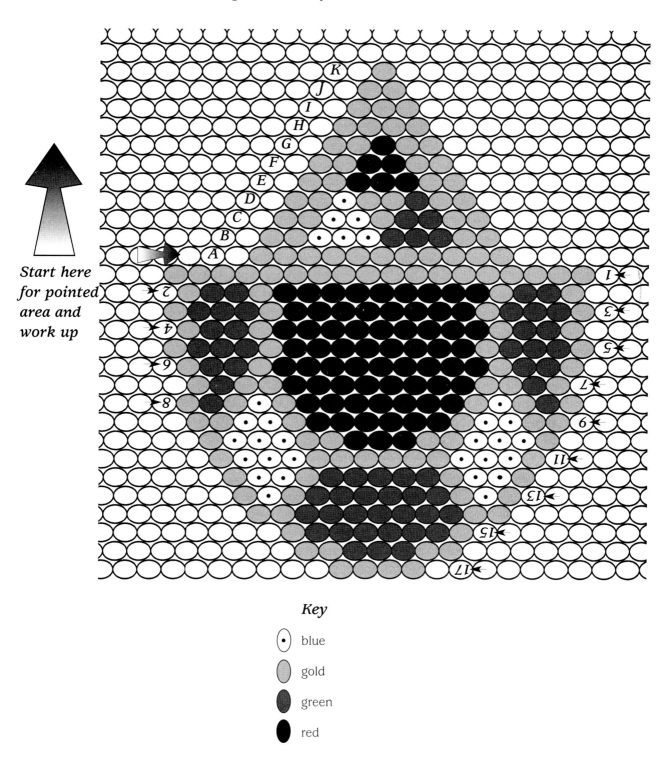

Start here for pointed area and work up

Key

- (•) blue
- gold
- green
- red

Snowflake Bracelet

refer to the colour photograph page 44

Winter is a time of magical delight, when the snow falls transforming our surroundings into sparkling whites and glacial blues and greens. Have your ever looked at a snowflake under a microscope? Each snowflake is unique and incredibly beautiful, they were the inspiration for this necklace and bracelet duo.

Finished size (fastened) 18.5cm (7 1/4")

Materials

- 18g cobalt blue seed beads Mill Hill 00020 *referred to as main colour*
- 4.5g pale green seed beads Mill Hill 02015
- 4.5g crystal seed beads Mill Hill 00161
- 4.5g pearl blue seed beads Mill Hill 02006
- Nymo® thread to match
- Two short beading needles
- Wax

Technique: Brick stitch

Instructions.

Row 1 – foundation row

Cut a 1.5m (5ft) length of thread and wax well. Thread a needle at each end, then pick up a main colour bead (cobalt blue), and position it in the centre of your thread (fig 1).

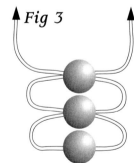

Fig 3

Repeat with the third bead (fig 3). Continue in this manner until 18 beads have been threaded.

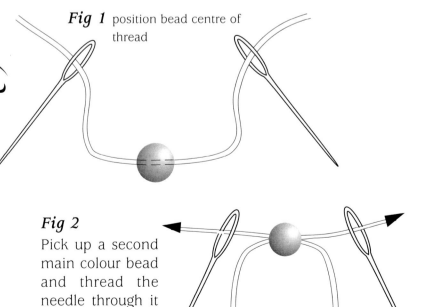

Fig 1 position bead centre of thread

Fig 2

Pick up a second main colour bead and thread the needle through it from each end (fig 2).

At the end of the row take each needle back through the second to last bead and then out through the last bead again (fig 4). This secures the end bead and makes it easier to start working Row 2. This is row one of the chart.

Row 2 Holding your beads with the two threads to the right hand side pick up the needle attached to the longer thread and turn beads to make sure this thread is coming out of the top of the end bead. Pick up a pale green bead and stitching towards yourself, bring the needle under the thread between the first and second bead of the foundation row and then go back up through the green bead (fig 5). Continue in this way following the chart to the end of the row. There are 17 beads in this row. The last bead is joined by taking the needle under the thread between the last two beads in the previous row.

Fig 4

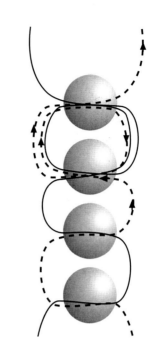

Fig 5   to start picking up
one bead

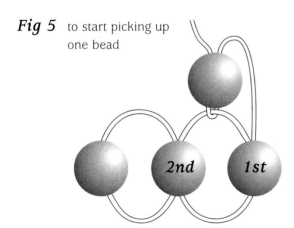

2nd   1st

Row 3 Pick up *two* beads before bringing the needle under the thread between the first and second bead of the previous row as before. (fig 6) Take the needle up through the second bead this time ensuring that the first bead is lying in the correct position. From this point on pick up one bead at a time, follow the chart for the correct beads to pick up. Attach the last bead by stitching under the thread at the end of the previous row (fig.7). This forms the delicately crenellated edge to the bracelet.

Fig 6
picking up two beads

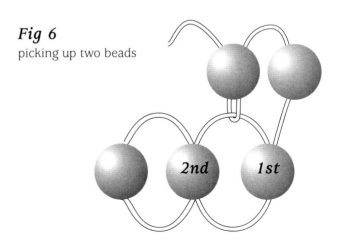

2nd   1st

Fig 7 stitching under the thread of the previous row

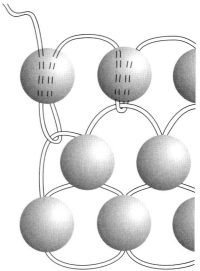

HANDY HINT

To start, if the line on the chart goes in, pick up one bead, if the line 'juts out' pick up two. When finishing if the line 'juts out' finish as shown in fig 7 if the line goes in the last stitch is between the last two beads of the previous row. There are 18 beads in every 'odd' row and 17 in every even row.

Changing Thread

You will probably need to change thread at least four times throughout the length of the bracelet. It is advisable to bring in a new thread when you have about 20cms (8") of the old thread left. Pick up a bead, take the thread down into the worked area and finish by working a clove hitch then thread your needle through some more beads, work another clove hitch, repeat about three times and then snip the thread end off.

Cut a new length of thread and remember to wax it well before you start. Bring the new thread up through different beads working clove hitches along the way and out through the last worked bead. Continue following the chart.

To Change the size of the Bracelet

Adjustments to the size of the bracelet can be made easily, to increase the length of the bracelet work complete snowflakes at each end of the bracelet, to decrease remove the half snowflakes at each end of the bracelet.

To fasten your bracelet

For simplicity a decorative, matching 8mm (3/8") bead can be used for the fastening. Take the thread in and out of the beads back along the last row to emerge at the fifth bead from the end add three seed beads for a stalk, add your decorative bead with a turning bead and rethread back down to secure in the main body of the bracelet. Repeat at the opposite end of the row.
Alternatively you can make the two beads see page 63.

To make the loops take the thread in and out of the beads back along the last row to emerge at the fifth bead from the end. String 22 beads (I used pale green) onto the thread and stitch into the sixth bead from the end. Work the thread in and out as if finishing with a couple of clove hitches and then go back and rethread along the 22 beads of the loop for extra strength. Finish off in the usual way. Repeat at the other end of the row for the second loop.

Following the Chart

Start at the bottom of the chart and work up. The arrow shows the starting point and for easy reference the initial rows are numbered. I find it helpful to rest a ruler on the row I am working, ticking off each row as I complete it. Then if interrupted it is easy to return to the correct position to continue. After the centre row, repeat the design in mirror image.

To Make Your Own Bead

Cut and wax a 1m (1yd) length of thread.

Pick up 14 beads, pass the needle through all the beads a second time forming a circle and tie a knot to secure. Place around the centre of a 5mm bead.

Work a row of peyote stitch above the central circle of beads, start by going through the first bead to the left of the knot and continue, pick up a bead, miss a bead and go through the next. On completion of the circle take the thread through all the beads you have just added and pull firmly to close them together, work a clove hitch to hold in place. Repeat this below the original central line of beads.

From this point on it is very fiddly as it is so small. To close in the two ends pick up a bead, miss two and go through the next. After that only two or three more beads are added, to fill the small space. Repeat for the other end.

When the beaded bead is completely covered weave your thread amongst the beads working two to three clove hitches as if fastening off. Pick up three beads for a little stalk and secure in the main body of the bracelet before returning back up the stalk to the bead and fastening off in the usual way. Finish the other thread end then repeat for the second bead fastener.

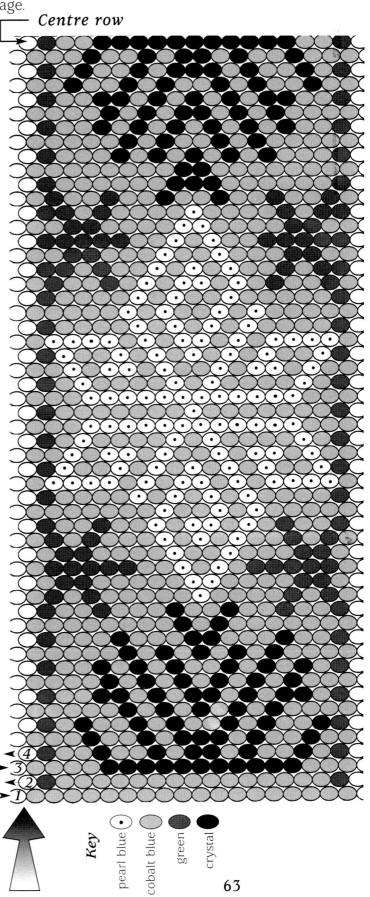

Centre row

Key: pearl blue, cobalt blue, green, crystal

63

Snowflake Necklace

refer to the colour photograph page 44

This necklace is made to complement the bracelet but it could also be worn most attractively on its own. It is made using the same techniques as the bracelet, but it has separate panels to give added interest to the design and these ensure that it sits beautifully flat at the base of the neck.

Materials

- 25g cobalt blue seed beads Mill Hill 00020
- 10g pale green seed beads Mill Hill 02015
- 5g pearl blue seed beads Mill Hill 02006
- 5g crystal seed beads Mill Hill 00161
- Nymo® thread to match
- Two short beading needles
- Silver findings
- Wax

Technique: Brick stitch

Instructions.

This necklace is make up of five panels, each stitched separately and then joined together on completion.
Refer to the chart for the starting position for each of the panels. The centre panel is inverted for ease of subsequent stitching. The neck strap is worked last so that adjustments can be made to vary the length to suit individual taste.

Centre Panel

Row 1 Foundation row Cut a 1.5m (5ft) length of thread and wax well. Thread a needle at each end, then pick up a pale green bead and position it in the centre of your thread (fig 1).

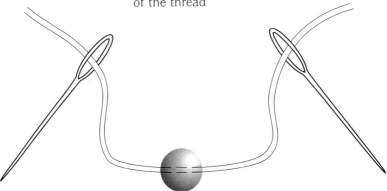

Fig 1 position bead in the centre of the thread

Fig 2

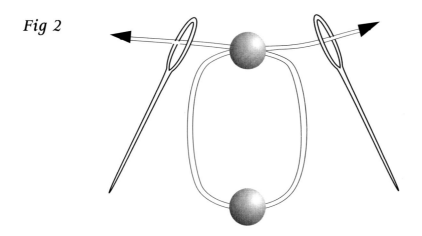

Pick up a second pale green bead and thread the needle through it from each end (fig 2). Repeat with the third bead (fig 3). Continue in this manner until 11 beads have been threaded five pale green first, then six cobalt blue. At the end of the row take each needle back through the second to last bead and then out through the last bead again (fig 4). This secures the end bead and makes it easier to start working Row 2. This is row one of the graph.

Fig 3   *Fig 4*

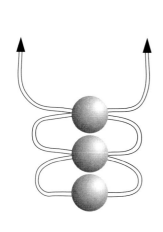

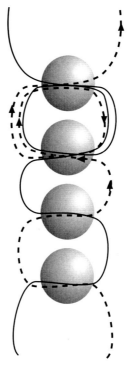

Row 2 Holding your beads with the two threads to the right hand side pick up the needle attached to the longer thread and turn your beads so that this thread is coming out of the top of the end bead. Start by picking up two cobalt blue beads and, stitching towards yourself, bring the needle under the thread between the first and second bead of the foundation row then take the needle back up through the second bead (fig 5) and pull into place, ensuring that the first bead sits in the correct position. Continue the row picking up one bead at a time, stitching under the thread and back up through the bead, being careful to keep the pattern correct, to the end of the row (fig 6). There are 11 beads in this row.

Fig 5
picking up two beads

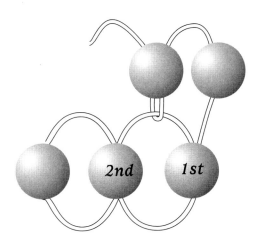

Fig 6 to start picking up one bead

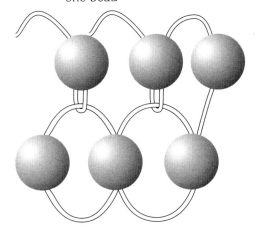

Row 3 Pick up two beads, a blue and a pale green bead then take the needle under the thread between the first and second bead of the previous row as before (fig 5). Continue, picking up one bead at a time following the chart, there are 12 beads in this row. The last bead in the row is attached in a different way to ensure a nice shape along the bottom edge of the panel, if not stitched in this way the beads are inclined to lie crookedly. When you come to the last bead in the row, pick up a bead, take your needle down the last bead of the previous row, back up through its neighbour and finally back up through the bead you picked up see shaded thread fig 7. Rows 3,5, 7, 9, 11 & 13 are finished in this way.

Fig 7

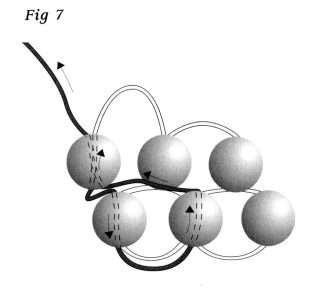

Continue stitching keeping the pattern correct adding a bead at *each end* of every *odd* row and adding *one* bead at the start of every *even* row until Row 13 which is the centre of the centre panel. After this row use the chart as a mirror image and decrease the shape along the lower edge. Follow the chart to the end of this panel but leave your thread end trailing ready to join the panels together when they are all completed, making sure your thread end emerges at the top edge of each of the panel pieces.

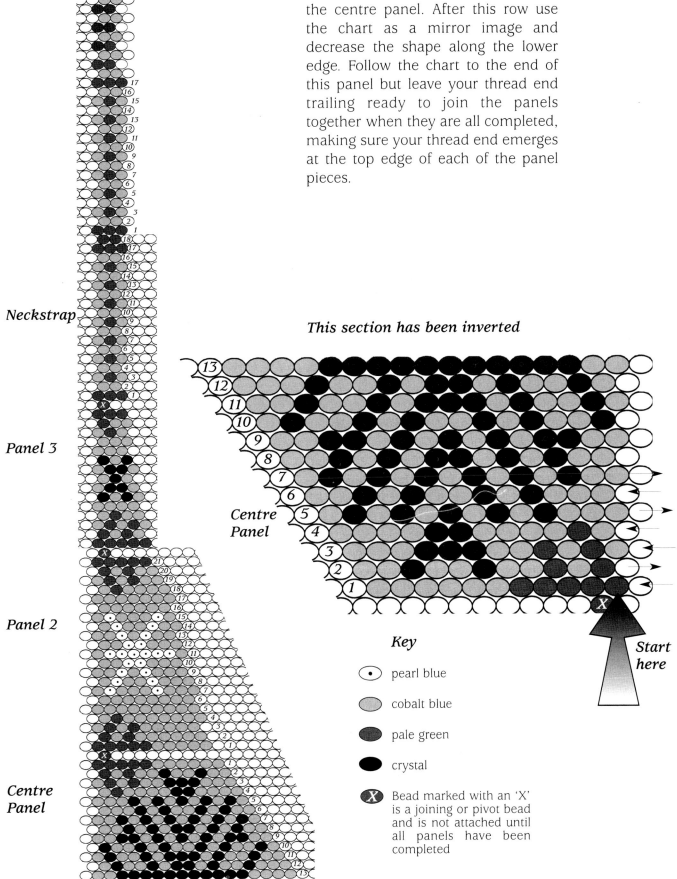

This section has been inverted

Neckstrap

Panel 3

Panel 2

Centre Panel

Centre Panel

Start here

Key

• pearl blue

cobalt blue

pale green

crystal

X Bead marked with an 'X' is a joining or pivot bead and is not attached until all panels have been completed

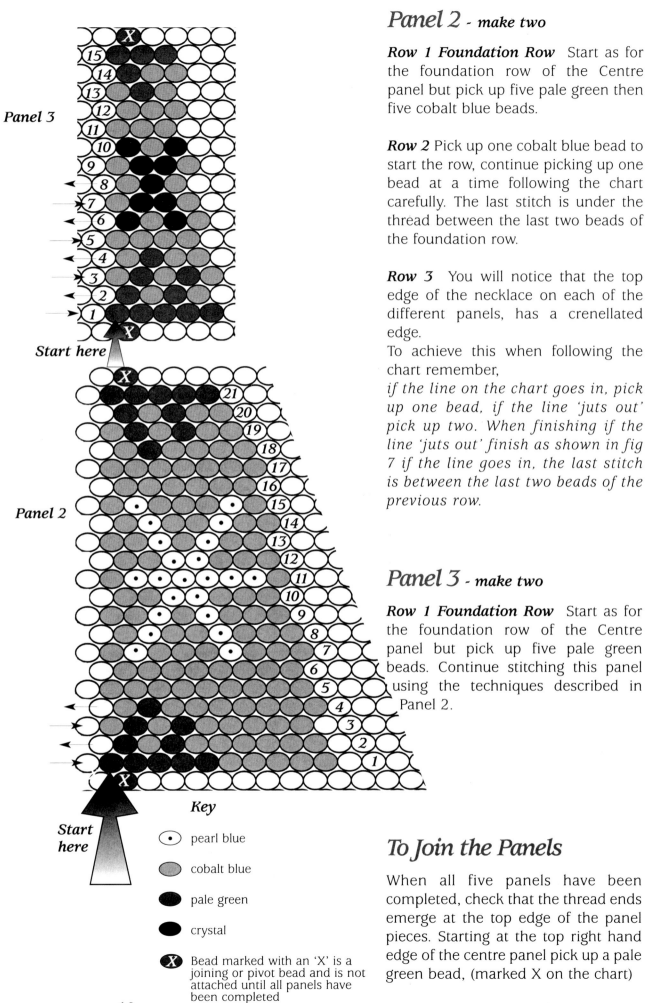

Panel 3

Start here

Panel 2

Start here

Key

⊙ pearl blue

⬭ cobalt blue

⬤ pale green

⬤ crystal

Ⓧ Bead marked with an 'X' is a joining or pivot bead and is not attached until all panels have been completed

Panel 2 - *make two*

Row 1 Foundation Row Start as for the foundation row of the Centre panel but pick up five pale green then five cobalt blue beads.

Row 2 Pick up one cobalt blue bead to start the row, continue picking up one bead at a time following the chart carefully. The last stitch is under the thread between the last two beads of the foundation row.

Row 3 You will notice that the top edge of the necklace on each of the different panels, has a crenellated edge.
To achieve this when following the chart remember,
if the line on the chart goes in, pick up one bead, if the line 'juts out' pick up two. When finishing if the line 'juts out' finish as shown in fig 7 if the line goes in, the last stitch is between the last two beads of the previous row.

Panel 3 - *make two*

Row 1 Foundation Row Start as for the foundation row of the Centre panel but pick up five pale green beads. Continue stitching this panel using the techniques described in Panel 2.

To Join the Panels

When all five panels have been completed, check that the thread ends emerge at the top edge of the panel pieces. Starting at the top right hand edge of the centre panel pick up a pale green bead, (marked X on the chart)

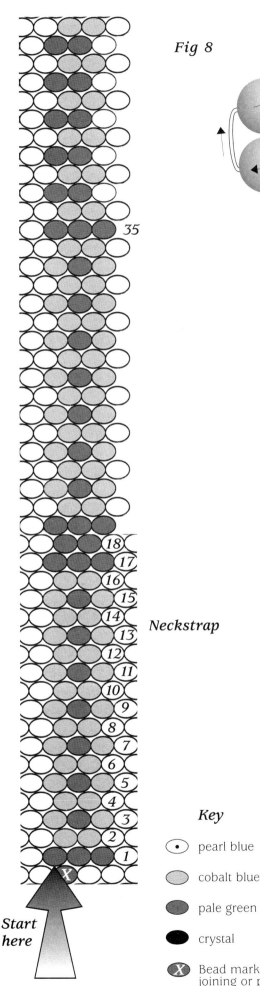

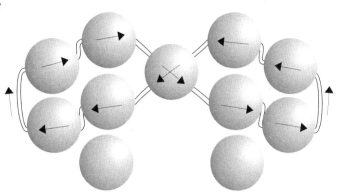

Fig 8

Neckstrap

35

18
17
16
15
14
13
12
11
10
9
8
7
6
5
4
3
2
1

X

Start here

Key

⊙ pearl blue

○ cobalt blue

⬭ pale green

⬬ crystal

Ⓧ Bead marked with an 'X' is a joining or pivot bead and is not attached until all panels have been completed

this bead will act as a link between the panels. Take your needle into the second to top bead in the next panel. Weave your thread around the beads in Panel 2 to secure the thread then return out of the top bead in that panel through 'X' and back into the second to top bead of the first panel. This keeps the pivot bead in the staggered position, maintaining the crenellated effect along the top edge of the necklace (fig 8).

Do this until the five front panels are joined. You are now ready to bead the remainder of the necklace.

The Neck Strap

Cut a 1.5m (5ft) length of thread and wax well. Start with three pale green beads and work following the chart in the usual manner for 35 rows finishing with three pale green beads. From this point on each row is only two beads long, alternating two blue then two pale green beads for 40 rows, or until desired length is gained. Attach one bead at a time for strength.

Attach clasp firmly weaving the thread end back through the neckstrap and finishing in the usual way. Repeat for the other side of the necklace. Join the neckstraps to the five already joined panels with a pivot bead.

Sunstone Pendant

refer to the colour photograph page 41

The necklace was inspired by the Japanese art of Kumihimo, the crafting of exotic silk braids. I thought it would be fun to twist a rope from beaded strands and so this design evolved. The 'beaded beads' are quite luxurious and add visual interest, texture and weight to the pendant as well as being enjoyable to make. They could of course be replaced by the purchase of three feature beads. There are two special beads in this necklace, the donut and a 3cm glass drop bead which I already had, I then chose a selection of seed and bigger beads for added interest to create a necklace that will attract attention wherever it goes!

Materials

- 1 x 5cm (2") diameter sun-stone donut
- 1 x 3cm (1 1/4") glass drop bead
- 1 x 1.5cm (5/8") spherical wooden bead*
- 2 x 1cm diameter x 1.5 cm long (1/2 x 5/8") oval wooden beads*
- 4 x 5mm (1/4") sun-stone beads
- 10 x 7mm(5/16") burnt orange foil filled glass beads
- 10 x 3mm (1/8") dark orange beads
- 4.5g antique gold seed beads Mill Hill 03039
- 2.6g frosted nutmeg seed beads Mill Hill 03038
- 4.5g copper seed beads Mill Hill 00330
- 4.5g root beer seed beads Mill Hill 02023
- 4.2g matt nutmeg seed beads Mill Hill 62023
- Nymo® thread to match
- wax
- 2 beading needles

*the 'beaded beads' are made over the top of these wooden beads, three feature beads could be purchased in their place if preferred.

Techniques: *Circular even count peyote including increasing and decreasing, Honeycomb stitch, Threading, Braiding.*

This necklace is made in stages. The 'beaded beads' are made first (Stage I). Stage II covers the section of the necklace which loops through the donut and includes the 3cm glass drop bead finishing with a loop of gold beads. In Stage III instructions are give for the two strands of seed beads which loop through the donut on the other side and Stage IV covers the braided section of the necklace. Read the instructions for each section carefully before you commence.

70

Stage 1 *The three 'beaded' beads*

Instructions

Oval bead *1 x 1.5cm oval wooden bead, copper seed beads, even count peyote stitch*

There are always different ways of doing things. I found it easier to begin at one end of this bead and work up. I also found putting the bead on a wooden skewer (or chopstick), so that it was held securely whilst I worked, most helpful. Copper seed beads were used throughout.

Cut and wax a 1.5m (5ft) length of thread. Pick up 10 copper seed beads and tie into a ring, about 20cms (8") from the end of the thread, allowing enough ease for another seed bead to be joined, position at the base of the bead. Working from right to left take the needle back through the first bead to the left of the knot, pick up a bead, miss a bead and go through the next bead to the end of the row. Pull the thread up tight so that the bead you are adding pushes the bead beneath it half way down the neighbouring beads. To move onto the next row take your needle through the first bead of the previous row then the first bead of the current row then continue in the usual way. (For detailed information on working peyote stitch refer to page 27.)

To increase - As you move up the bead you will find you need to increase. Do this by picking up two beads and easing them into a space (fig 1).

Fig 1 increasing

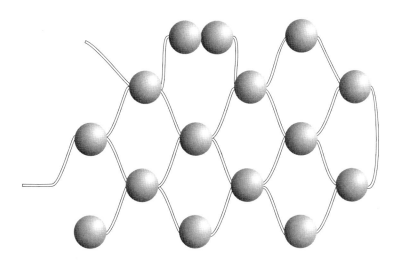

To decrease - take the needle through two beads in the previous row without adding one in between (fig 2).

Fig 2 decreasing

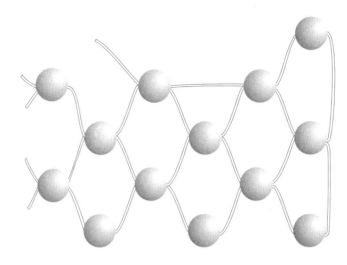

Continue working increasing or decreasing as required to cover the bead. Always pull the beads tightly together so as not to leave any gaps. When the under bead is covered thread the needle back through all the beads in the last row then pull firmly to draw the beads around the opening. Finish thread in the usual manner.

Fig 3

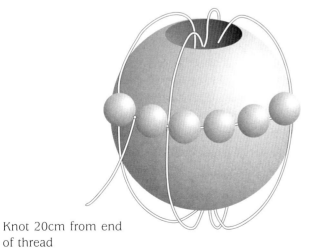

Knot 20cm from end of thread

Spherical bead *1.5cm spherical bead, frosted nutmeg and gold seed beads, even count peyote stitch*

Cut and wax a 1.5m (5ft) length of thread. Pick up 30 frosted nutmeg beads and tie in a ring around the centre of the wooden bead, knot 20cm (8") from one end of the thread (fig 3). Then take the thread down to the base of the bead, up through the middle and back down to the centre string, work one clove hitch. Repeat so that there are four vertical threads to hold the central horizontal thread in position working a clove hitch each time the vertical thread joins the horizontal thread.

To make it easier to work on the bead push it onto a chopstick or skewer to hold the bead firm.

Working from the centre upwards, work one row of peyote stitch using frosted nutmeg beads and the next row alternating one gold bead and one frosted nutmeg.

Decreasing

To keep the beads snugly against the wooden bead you will need to decrease. This is done by taking the needle through two beads in the previous row without adding one in between, (fig 2). Work the remaining rows using the frosted nutmeg and gold beads selected randomly decreasing as required to cover the bead completely. This will take approximately four rows. My final row had only six beads. Take your needle through the six drawing them in around the centre hole, work two or three clove hitches before weaving your thread back through the beads to the centre.

Turn the bead over and repeat to cover the second half of the bead in the same way. Finish threads in the usual way.

Oval Honeycomb stitch bead *1 x 1.5 cm oval wooden bead, gold and frosted nutmeg seed beads*

This stitch has a much more open weave and the colour of the wooden bead below can plainly be seen. Be careful to choose a complementary colour for the base bead or paint it to match, allowing it to dry thoroughly before beading over it.

The first three rows are worked without the bead, then the bead is placed inside the shape created.

Row 1 Cut and wax a 1m (1yd) length of thread. Pick up six gold seed beads and take your needle back through the first bead 'A' to form a circle. Leave a 30cm (12") length of thread at the beginning (fig 4).

Fig 4

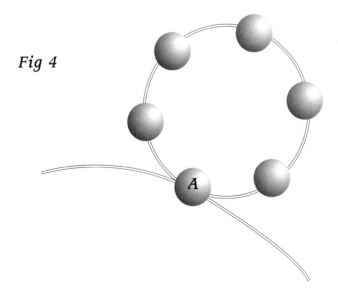

Row 2 Pick up two gold beads, miss a bead and go through the next bead. Repeat twice. This takes you back through your start bead a second time (fig 5)

Fig 5

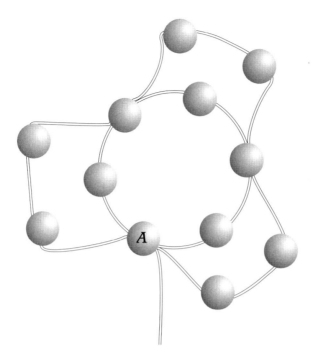

Row 3 Pick up three beads, gold, frosted nutmeg, gold and instead of going through a bead stitch *under* the thread between the two gold beads (fig 6). Now pull the 30cm (12") length of thread firmly from the left and the thread in the needle firmly from the right and the beads will, with a little encouragement, form a little 'vessel' shape with the beads coming forward to form a hollow tube which is closed at the base. Slip the oval wooden bead into the shape insert a skewer so that you can hold this whilst working on the bead and continue.

Fig 6   stitch under the thread between the two gold beads

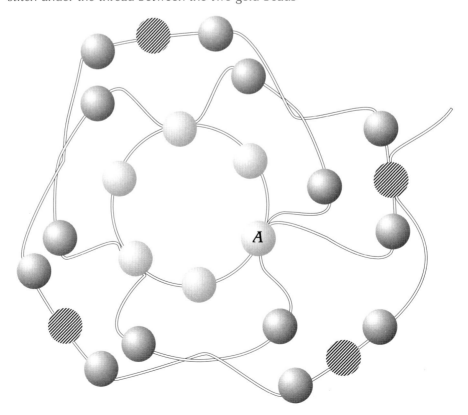

Row 4 Work another row picking up three beads (gold, frosted nutmeg, gold) and go through the nutmeg bead from the previous row.

As you work up the shape you will need to increase and then decrease. To increase pick up five beads (two gold, one frosted nutmeg, two gold) always going through the central nutmeg bead from the previous row. To decrease pick up three or two beads. Take your needle back through the final six once more drawing the end in as tightly as possible around the bead. Finish thread ends in the usual way.

Stage II

This section of the necklace loops through the donut and includes the 3cm (1 1/4") glass drop bead finishing with a loop of gold seed beads.

Cut and wax a 1.5m (5ft) length of thread. Tie on a keeper bead 20cm (8") from one end of the thread, then pick up three gold seed beads, sun-stone bead, two gold seed beads, another sun-stone bead, two more gold seed beads, a sun-stone bead and then 24 gold seed beads. Thread these through the middle of the sun-stone donut and take the needle back through the first *three gold seed beads,* remove the keeper bead. This forms a loop around the donut.

Pick up a burnt orange bead and three nutmeg seed beads. Repeat twice.
Pick up eight frosted nutmeg seed beads, take your needle back through the third bead forming a little loop and then pick up two more frosted nutmeg seed beads (fig. 7).
Repeat from * - * with root beer, copper and gold beads.

Pick up the glass drop and then four gold seed beads, stitching through the first gold seed bead again to form a little collar for the last sun-stone bead to sit upon.

Pick up 30 gold seed beads, these form a loop when you stitch back through the sun-stone bead, around the collar through the glass drop *and back through all the beads to the beginning for extra strength.* Finish off thread ends securely in the usual way.

Fig 7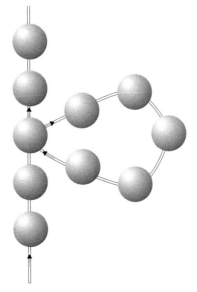

Stage III

The two strands of seed beads which loop through the donut on the other side.

Cut and wax a 1.5m (5ft) length of thread. Tie on a keeper bead. Pick up three matt nutmeg seed beads and one copper seed bead 38 times. The beads will measure 23cms (9"). Position the beads centrally on your length of thread and take one end through the sun-stone donut. Remove the keeper bead and tie the thread ends together *right up close to the beads* (making sure the thread ends are about the same length) so the donut is secure.

Cut and wax a second length of thread, 1.6m (5ft 6") long. Tie on a keeper bead. Pick up three root beer seed beads then three frosted nutmeg seed beads. Repeat the pattern until it measures 26cms (10 1/2") long. As before, thread one end through the sun-stone donut, remove the keeper bead and tie *right up close to the beads,* leaving the remaining ends equal length to each other. This strand is longer so it hangs like a chain rather than taking the weight of the pendant.

Now, thread the four thread ends in two needles and take all the threads through the circular beaded bead, two burnt orange beads, the honeycomb beaded bead, another burnt orange bead and finally the copper peyote bead. Unthread the ends and separate, there are four separate threads each 55cm (22") in length.

Stage IV *the braided section of the necklace*

In this stage, *thread 35 cm (14") of beads on each strand.* Note the strands are threaded differently. It is a good idea to make a little catch stitch like a keeper stitch, around the final bead so the beads do not move during the next step.
Strand One gold seed beads.
Strand Two copper seed beads.
Strand Three alternate three matt nutmeg seed beads with one frosted nutmeg.
Strand Four the final strand, is threaded with root beer seed beads with nine dark orange beads interspersed randomly along its length.

Once you have threaded all four strands you are ready to braid them together. You can do this by yourself as the braid is not particularly tight but it is easier if someone else holds the oval 'beaded' bead for you. Lay the work on the table and spread the strands out, almost like a cross (fig 8). The copper and gold should be one pair of opposites, the nutmeg and root beer the second pair. Taking care not to lose where you are, cross

---

HANDY HINT

A simple but very attractive necklace could be made by just braiding four strings of beads

---

left strand to the right and right strand to the left, then top strand to the bottom and bottom strand to the top. Repeat from * - * until the threads are braided together. The tighter you do it the firmer your cord will be. This creates a four sided braid which is particularly luxurious with the mingled warm tones of the beads. Continue braiding to the end of the strands and knot the pairs together, being careful to remove the catch stitches first. This is how a Zopf bread loaf is folded in Switzerland.

Fig 8

copper

root beer

nutmeg

gold

Take all the ends through a dark orange bead to bunch them together. Thread one pair of strands onto a needle and pick up 3 copper seed beads and a burnt orange bead. Repeat three more times and finish with three seed beads. Go back through the dark orange bead and finish the ends separately in the usual way amongst the braided sections of the necklace. Thread the second pair of thread ends and go through all the same beads to strengthen before fastening off in the same way.

You have now completed a beautiful art form to add to your wardrobe. I hope you enjoy wearing it.

Fig 9   after first crossover

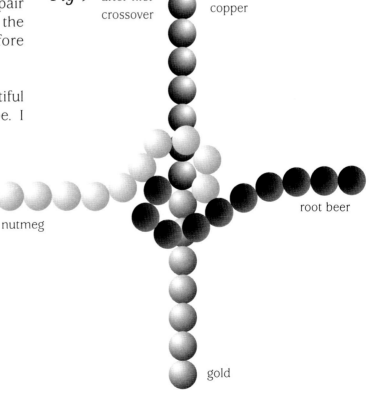

copper

nutmeg

root beer

gold

Use chart this way for Circular Brick Stitch

Use chart this way for Peyote Stitch

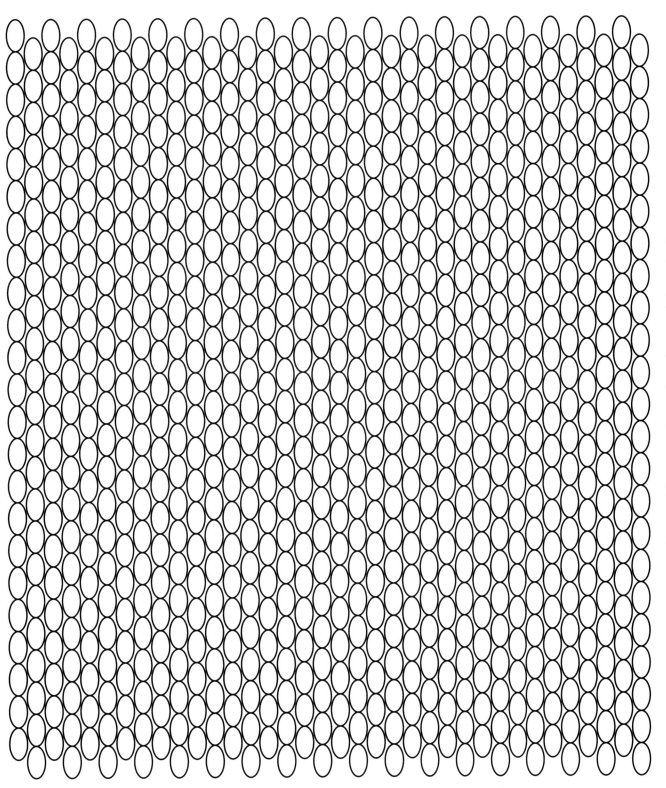

Use chart this way for Circular Brick Stitch

Use chart this way for Peyote Stitch

For New Zealand readers - all beads are available in New Zealand.

Contact us for details